A RUNNING
START

*How Play, Physical Activity
and Free Time Create a Successful Child*

★

RAE PICA

MARLOWE & COMPANY
NEW YORK

A Running Start:
How Play, Physical Activity and Free Time Create a Successful Child

Copyright © 2006 by Rae Pica

Published by
Marlowe & Company
An Imprint of Avalon Publishing Group, Incorporated
245 West 17th Street • 11th Floor
New York, NY 10011-5300

AVALON
publishing group incorporated

Library of Congress Cataloging-in-Publication Data is available

ISBN-10: 1-56924-284-4
ISBN-13: 978-1-56924-284-1
9 8 7 6 5 4 3 2 1

Designed by Maria E. Torres
Printed in the United States of America

This book is dedicated to my mother,
Eleanor Pica-Merrill,
from whom I acquired my love of dance,
and to the memory of my father,
Raymond Pica, for his sense of humor.

Contents

Introduction

This book is about raising a successful child/human being. That seems simple enough. But it gets complicated when we consider that there's been a shift in our collective thinking as to how success is achieved.

Many parents have been led to believe that if their child excels in school and in sports *at a very early age*, she or he will grow up to be a more successful adult. By getting a head start, their children will have an advantage in what they perceive to be a highly competitive world. The thinking goes:

- The road to success is through scoring goals and acing tests (the child with the most blue ribbons and the highest grades wins).
- By "accelerating" their children's development, parents can ensure a more successful future for them.
- That as parents, they—and they alone—are responsible for determining their children's futures.
- If they don't do "whatever it takes," their children will not succeed.

I call these well-intentioned but often misplaced expectations the "superkid" myths—defining success not in terms of happiness, but in terms of being better and having more than the other guy. The result of these myths is that no longer can children just *be*; they must *do*. Childhood today has become a dress rehearsal for adulthood, and, for many children, life has become a great big competition. A race to walk and talk earlier than the other infants. To get into the best preschool. To be a star at Little League. To participate in the most activities. To excel. To win. To be the *most* "above-average" child in the history of children. To have a résumé, upon entrance into first grade, that will guarantee a place in the best high school, the best college, and later, in the best corporation/law firm/medical practice.

But what are kids really winning when they're losing out on childhood? There are millions of adults out there who are tired of the rat race, and they didn't start racing until they were at least in their twenties. How long can today's children be expected to love life when they start racing before they're even toddling?

* * *

When most of us think back to our childhoods, playing is probably the first thing that comes to mind. We played tag and hide-and-seek. We played "make-believe": cops and robbers, mommies and daddies, movie star. We formed pickup games. We followed the trail of a caterpillar or worker ant.

I remember recess twice a day, during which my friend Kathy and I choreographed dances to Beatles' songs, performing them on the playground for the other kids. I remember waking up on summer mornings with a tingle of excitement and an irrepressible urge to get outside. I have fond memories of learning to turn cartwheels, crushing milkweed pods with a rock as we acted out being "pilgrims," and *trees*: a picnic under a weeping willow, a pear tree in the backyard, getting stuck in a neighbor's because I could climb up but couldn't climb back down.

Those were the days—unlike any others I've had since or will ever have again. Even vacations can't begin to compare. Okay, it may not have been like living at Disneyland; even as children we had occasional worries, but if you're like me, the magic and the wonder are what you retained. And having that once-in-a-lifetime chance to be a child is what sustains you now, when life isn't always magical or wonderful.

Because we imagined creatures in the clouds, we have the imagination to prepare a meal from a refrigerator full of leftovers. Because we mastered riding a bike, turning cartwheels, and climbing trees (eventually getting both up and down), we have the confidence to tackle technology or tennis. We invented games when there was nobody to play with and learned resourcefulness and how to handle solitude. We invented games with our friends, creating and re-creating the rules, and learned the fine arts of cooperation, conflict resolution, and problem solving. Because the lives of today's children are so structured, and because I've seen free play disappearing from the landscape of childhood, I worry that children now have too few opportunities to acquire these important life skills. That is the primary reason that I decided to write *A Running Start*.

Over the 27-year period that I've worked as a children's physical activity specialist, I have watched educational priorities wax and wane. When I first began consulting, little was known about the role of movement in the learning process, but at least educators understood that young children learn best through play. Today, we have considerable research proving that they were right and, moreover, that movement, play, and physical activity contribute to brain and intellectual development. Despite this, educators too often tell me they don't have *time* for movement and play because there are so many standards to meet and tests for which they must prepare the children.

This shift in educational priorities—from active learning to seatwork and high-stakes testing—was a gradual one. But with the implementation of No Child Left Behind, seatwork and high-stakes testing became the norm. As a result, recess and physical education—play and physical activity in the schools—are in danger of disappearing.

At the same time that educational priorities were shifting, parental priorities were, too. Children were being enrolled in more and more organized activities, and childhood itself became an exercise in goal attainment. Achievement came to supersede play, which meant that this important aspect of childhood was also disappearing in homes.

My colleagues and I have watched these trends in disbelief and dismay. I've written extensively on the importance of movement, play, and physical activity in the lives of young children; and I've traveled the country spreading the "movement message." However, most of my work has been directed toward educators and others who work with young children. Recently I realized, through my conversations with both teachers and parents, that I must also spread the message to those who *live* with young children. My hope is that if I can help parents better understand the priorities of childhood, they'll make the needed changes at home and require that the schools similarly embrace these priorities. My hope is that *A Running Start* will prompt a shift back in the other direction toward play and the recognition that:

- especially in childhood, the process is more important than the product
- having fun is more beneficial to a child than winning
- trying one's best *because* it's fun prompts children to stick with it and motivates them to improve their skills
- enjoying learning is more important than learning to regurgitate what a teacher feeds in.

What's my definition of success? The one I offer in *A Running Start* doesn't involve a financial element. Rather, when I think of success, I envision someone who's truly happy with life—a well-rounded individual who has the bases covered in all three developmental domains: intellectual, physical, and social/emotional.

For example, when I consider "academic" success, I imagine someone who's adept at problem solving, able to handle whatever questions and challenges life throws her way. She's also a lifelong learner: someone who so enjoys the process of learning that she never tires of discovering more of what the world has to offer. She may love to read, to hear people's stories, or to otherwise uncover the hows and whys of the world around her. Simply put, her education hasn't stopped just because she's no longer in school.

When I consider "athletic" success, it's no more and no less than someone who's physically active and physically fit, whose early experiences were positive enough to encourage him to keep moving and stay healthy. So, now we have a lifelong learner who's also active for life.

And then there's the personal/social aspect. Here I envision an individual with confidence who relates well with others. Someone with good character and heart, whom other people admire for who they are, not how many toys they have.

Taken together, the three domains—intellectual, physical, and social/emotional—are what we in the early childhood field refer to as the "whole child" (or, as I also like to call it: the "thinking, moving, feeling" child). The goal of early childhood education has long been to help children develop in all three of these areas, and I'm a huge proponent of the concept. But, as I remind parents and professionals in my presentations, it's important to understand that these three domains overlap and interrelate. Children cannot learn or experience something in one domain without it impacting the other two.

You'll see, therefore, as you read this book, that there is overlap and interrelatedness among the chapters here as well. For example, although it may come as a surprise to you, physical activity contributes a great deal to children's cognitive/intellectual development. Similarly, children who are physically skilled tend to be more popular among their peers, meaning there's a connection between physical and social development. Even the relaxation I prescribe for personal success, in chapter 8, has ramifications beyond the obvious: Because it stimulates creative- and critical-thinking skills, among other things, relaxation plays a role in cognitive development. And these are just a few examples.

* * *

A Running Start takes a close look at the misinformation parents have been fed, particularly in the areas of education and sports participation. The myths explored in chapter 1, Keeping It Real: How Kids Really Learn, are related to how children learn and what truly determines intelligence: that children must be encouraged to learn, and that babies and young children need gadgets and gear for the best brain development. In reality, children are born with a desire to learn; and good, old-fashioned play and movement are the best contributors to brain development.

Too often, children are enrolled in organized sports long before they're developmentally ready. Most parents aren't aware that such skills as eye-hand and eye-foot coordination aren't fully developed until age nine or ten, so a young child isn't likely to master connecting bat to ball, foot to ball, or stick to puck. To enroll or not to enroll? Chapter 2, Ready or Not, Here Come Organized Sports, will help you make informed choices about the best time to sign your child up.

Chapter 3, Helping Your Child Master Movement, asserts that the way to ensure success in sports—and a lifelong love of physical activity—is not for children to dive right in but to first practice and refine the fundamentals. These ABCs of movement are as essential to physical activity as the alphabet is to reading.

Chapter 4, The Real Standards for "Smart," is devoted to the myth that standardized tests are an accurate measurement of a child's intelligence, when in fact there are many kinds of intelligence and standardized tests fail to measure most of them. This chapter will help you discover not how smart your child is, but how your child is smart.

Chapter 5, Is Your Child Playing Enough at School?, covers

another two myths: that (1) An early emphasis on "academics" will ensure a more successful future, and (2) The sole purpose of a child's education is to teach reading, writing, and 'rithmetic. I believe it is only when you understand what really matters in your child's formal education that you can stand up to the administrators and advocate for what's best for him. This chapter helps promote that understanding.

As the title indicates, chapter 6, Finding the Right Organized Activity Program, will help you find the right, developmentally appropriate, organized programs for your child, while keeping expectations real.

Finally, the last three chapters address what it means to foster personal and social success. Chapter 7, You've Gotta Have Heart: Why Compassion Matters More than Competition, asks such questions as: What values do we want to instill in our children? What characteristics are truly important to a child's future? And does the competitive nature of today's society promote those characteristics and values, or does it have the opposite effect? We'll explore the myth that being able to compete in a dog-eat-dog world is the most important trait for a child to have.

In chapter 8, Finding Creatures in the Clouds: The Value of Downtime, I'll tackle the mistaken notion that downtime is wasted time. Contrary to current popular belief, ample time to just dabble or "do nothing" are critical to a child's present and future health and success.

Finally, chapter 9, Getting Back on Track: Family First, contends that the time you spend together as a family will contribute more to your child's running start than any jumpstart you might hope to give him in academics or athletics. We'll then explore the power that parents have to make the changes that can make a difference for their children. At the other extreme, however, the final section of this chapter will look at the ways in which you must concede the power: by simply relaxing and trusting that your child is going to turn out just fine.

Throughout the nine chapters, you'll find plenty of boxes called "Play & Learn Activities," in which I'll provide concrete suggestions and fun activities to help you and your child reach for the realities rather than the myths.

* * *

I don't mean for the title of this book, *A Running Start*, to give the impression that it's intended to help you give your child a jumpstart on the other kids, or to help you raise a child who is superior to all others. Although I do agree that a parent contributes to her child's development and future, I also firmly believe that pushing a child to develop ahead of her inborn timetable does harm. *A Running Start*, therefore, isn't about the pressure to hurry children into adulthood. Rather, it refers literally to what I feel is the *natural* way you can give your child the best possible start in life: by letting your child be a child. By letting him run and jump and play—or, if desired, do "nothing."

It's an old-fashioned contention, I know: that the best way to give your child a running start is to take time out to play. It saddens me that such a belief is actually considered controversial today. But the belief certainly isn't mine alone; educators, child development specialists, and the research agree. In fact, as this book was being written, the American Academy of Pediatrics issued a report contending that children need more old-fashioned free play. Titled "The Importance of Play in Promoting Healthy Child Development and Maintaining Strong Parent-Child Bonds," the report stresses that play is far more beneficial to children than overscheduling and enrichment activities.

Authentic play, fun, and free time will best help your children achieve their life's goals. By allowing children their childhood, we give them the greatest running start of all. For the children's sakes, it's time for the superkid madness to stop. Perhaps you never got caught up in it, but you're feeling as though you're all alone in the wilderness. Perhaps you did get caught up in it but are beginning to consider (or need some convincing) that life on the fast track isn't the way childhood is supposed to be. *A Running Start*—its information, ideas, and support—is for you.

1 ★ Keeping It Real
How Kids Really Learn

"We own everything electronic that's educational . . . .There's only one thing better than having a baby, and that's having a smart baby."

—(Naira, mother of an eleven-month old, quoted in the *New York Times*)

If you're a parent today, no doubt you've been led to believe that your child might fall hopelessly behind—or, perhaps worse, might be only as smart as the next kid—without a little help from "acceleration" materials.

The subject of "superkids" gets plenty of press these days. *Time* recently devoted the better part of an issue—complete with cover story—on how to raise one. *Newsweek* featured a story about overscheduled children, called "Busy Around the Clock." Articles with titles like

"Whatever Happened to Play?," "Pushing Children Too Hard," and "Are You Over-Scheduling Your Kids?" regularly show up in print media and on the Internet. Superkids are even a popular topic among "mommy blogs."

What are superkids? Some people call them *overscheduled;* others refer to them as *pushed* or *hurried.* Some speak of the practice of creating superkids as *scheduled hyperactivity.* Most agree the practice is today's status symbol among families. In short, a superkid is a child who is pressured by parents and by society in general to do too much too soon. Parents are determined not only to have their young children do well but also to have them do better than the other kids. It all starts with how smart they are—from the basics, like how early they learn to recite their ABCs and count to fifty, to the complex, like how many foreign languages they can speak before they're three years old. From the moment of birth, the race is on.

In today's superkid culture, childhood is too often being seen not as a treasured, unique period in a person's lifespan, but as a dress rehearsal for adulthood. Somehow, childhood has evolved from being about play, discovery, and wonder to being solely about achievement—filling out a résumé that will impress even the most unimpressionable of college admissions officers (not to mention preschool administrators—but we'll get to that). Today, it's no longer enough for children to do well; they're also expected to excel. Our littlest human beings have become human *doings,* with parents keeping their children so busy that the little ones need PDAs to monitor their schedules.

To accomplish superstardom, parents are spending millions of dollars on "educational products" in the form of flashcards, videos/DVDs, and computer software. In 2000, over just a nine-month period, parents and caregivers spent about $11 million on software for babies and toddlers alone. Among their choices is JumpStart Baby, for children nine months to two years old, which, according to a SuperKids Educational Software Review, is "crucial . . . in the development of beginning critical thinking skills." The review then goes on to say, "Although interaction is minimal, it is enough to give the child a sense of control. With adult supervision, Baby can learn to tap lightly on the keyboard keys, or click the mouse when Teddy asks, and experience the result of these actions." It doesn't mention how this is related to critical thinking. (Children's Software Review cites being good at waiting and following directions—two skills even preschoolers can't be expected to be skilled at—as necessary for this software.)

A quick scan of the Internet displays other "educational" offerings. There's a Brainy Baby video called "Baby Brainy Peek-A-Boo" that can teach little ones the joys of this age-old game (no parents required). For $99.99 parents can buy a twenty DVD Baby Einstein set. Possibilities here include "Baby da Vinci from Head to Toe," providing "baby's first introduction to their eyes, ears, hands, feet, and more" (evidently, as a substitute for such experiences as "Where Is Thumbkin?" or "This Little Piggy") and "Baby Neptune Discovering Water" (which I always imagined babies discovered at bath time or in a kiddie pool). Many of these DVDs feature Spanish, English, and French language tracks "for added learning."

Speaking of languages, parents can also purchase flashcards to give their children the edge in language learning. Spanish flashcards seem to be the most popular, but you can also get them in French, Chinese, and Japanese. And if improving a child's English is the goal, there are plenty of early learning tools for that purpose as well. Parents can buy a set of cards for every letter of the alphabet. The set for the letter *d*, for example, ensures that children become "familiar" with desks, dogs, dolls, and doors, among other things—objects already found in most every home.

But do these two-dimensional tools offer children what they need to learn? The question perhaps should be: is a jumpstart on learning really necessary?

It's true that brain development and intelligence are a complex mix of nature and nurture—and that we humans do have the ability to enhance what nature gave us and, thus, our potential. Studies show that certain areas of the brain—like those controlling our breathing and our heartbeat—are "prewired," but that other areas are ultimately determined by our experiences. And we've been made aware that enriched environments can improve on those experiences and, as such, on a child's brain development.

★ SUPERKID ALERT! ★

Myth: To promote the "best" brain development, infants and young children need the latest gadgets and gear.

Reality: Old-fashioned play and physical experiences offer the best opportunities for brain development.

An enriched environment is simply one in which children are touched and talked to and given ample opportunity to move and explore. However, this idea has been taken to the extreme. Marketers have convinced us that "enriched" means far more than what it actually does. Parents have been left with the impression that they are the sole architects of their children's brains, and that if not "designed" in the early years, their brains—and thus their futures— are left to chance.

This notion has created no end of confusion. Parents have been told that because children master language acquisition most efficiently in the first few years of life, foreign-language videos will help them become multilingual. (Otherwise kids might miss the opportunity!) Because children will have to ace the math portion of the SATs, parents purchase software and flash numerical cards while their children are still in diapers, with the hope of creating mathematical whizzes. (Otherwise children may never be accepted into an Ivy League college!) And because technology has become so integral to our lives and work, parents have been encouraged to purchase infant "lapware" (a new market of software for babies that requires parents to hold their little ones on their lap) and enroll their toddlers in computer classes. (Otherwise they might grow up not knowing how to operate one!) The enormous pressure—the fear that your child won't be smart enough—is enough to make a person wonder how anyone handles being a parent these days. A perception has been created, from numerous sources, that it's a highly competitive world out there—and that flashcards, videos, and early computer literacy will help ensure a child is "smart enough."

REALITY CHECK ✓

As Joan Almon writes in *All Work and No Play:* "Children are not machines. You cannot simply add more fuel and speed them up. They are governed by internal processes that are sometimes called 'the laws of child development.' We cannot ignore these natural developmental timetables without doing serious harm to children."

The reality is that all children are born with an innate desire to learn and discover. And rather than determining destiny, abilities have a way of leveling out in children. Your child may read earlier than any of your neighbors' children, but the other kids will have caught up by third grade; and at that point it really won't matter who read first. There's no research that shows children who read earlier end up reading *better*. Furthermore, there is evidence that hurrying children can do more harm than good. Noted educator Lillian Katz has pointed out that there are short-term advantages when three- to five-year-olds are given formal instruction but considerable disadvantages in the long term. According to a study by the International Association for the Evaluation of Educational Achievement, reading literacy was the highest in those countries where reading instruction began at 6.3 years of age. Boys, in particular, had difficulties when required to begin reading formally at age five.

In *The Hurried Child* noted child development specialist David Elkind writes, "Many children acquire learned helplessness . . . when they are confronted with . . . tasks that are too difficult for their level of ability." He contends that pressuring children can lead to psychosomatic illnesses, decreased interest in learning, lack of autonomy, and a tendency to worry, among other problems. Elkind adds, "Hurrying children into adulthood violates the sanctity of life by giving one period priority over another."

Succumbing to the lure of "earlier is better," urging your child to learn in unnatural ways for which he's not developmentally ready, you may unintentionally create a kid-unfriendly environment. At the very least, just by virtue of spending the majority of his time in a two-dimensional world, your child will be deprived of authentic play and social interaction. Rather than boosting abilities, this may actually contribute to problems with language development, a lack of creativity and problem-solving skills, attention difficulties, weight problems, impaired motor development, vision problems, lack of social skills, and excessive stress.

★ SUPERKID ALERT! ★

Myth: Children have to be encouraged to learn.

Reality: Children are "hardwired" with a craving for discovery and learning. Forcing it—as well-intentioned as it might be—may unwittingly create a child who learns to dislike learning.

Keeping It Real with Baby

A baby's brain and intellectual development rely on nurturing relationships, the sound of your voice, and physical contact. Leading brain researcher Dr. Marian Diamond contends that it is emotional support and language from parents that helps babies and toddlers reach optimal development. Dr. Lise Eliot, author of *What's Going on in There?* says that touch "has a surprisingly potent influence over [babies'] physical growth, emotional well-being, cognitive potential, and even their overall health." And Dr. Sharon Heller, in *The Vital Touch,* agrees: "Every caress, stroke, hug, squeeze, and playful game; all the rocking, swaying, swinging, spinning; all the sights, sounds, smells, and tastes in our [child's] world—all feed [the] need for sensory input and spark the neurons in her brain to grow and branch out to encompass other neurons." Additionally, when you talk to and lovingly play with your baby, you're providing him with a sense of security and trust. He feels wanted and loved and worthy. All of this contributes to the child's physical, social/emotional, and cognitive development—the "whole child."

I'm sure that just as parents have done throughout the ages, you've rocked, jiggled, bounced, and walked your baby. You intuitively knew that such motions soothed your child. What you probably didn't know was why: Along with touch, a baby's developed-at-birth vestibular system—the body's sense of movement and balance—conveys sensation, calming the child. This motion and sensation also promote early brain development. Along with touch, a baby's developed-at-birth vestibular system—the body's sense of movement and balance—conveys sensation, calming the child.

Games like peekaboo and patty-cake have survived for generations because they offer so much of what a baby needs. Peekaboo promotes bonding through eye contact and laughter, and it teaches the child about object permanence (things don't disappear simply because we can't see them). Patty-cake provides physical touch and gives baby a chance to cross the vertical midline of the body, which, like crawling, requires the two hemispheres of the brain to communicate across the corpus callosum (the matter connecting the two hemispheres). It also helps develop eye-hand coordination. When you play "This Little Piggy" with your child's toes, you're again offering physical touch and laughter, with a healthy dose of body awareness thrown in. Holding your baby and gently swaying—preferably skin to skin—provides vestibular (motion awareness) stimulation and soothes *both* of you. Even making funny faces contributes to your child's development. When baby imitates, she is learning through observation and acquiring communication skills.

Early movement experiences, in fact, are considered essential to the neural stimulation (the use-it-or-lose-it principle involved in keeping or pruning brain cells, or neurons) needed for healthy brain development. An infant's brain is chock-full of neurons at birth. Over time each of these brain cells can form as many as fifteen thousand connections (synapses) with other brain cells. And it is during the first three years of life that most of these connections are made. Synapses not used often enough are eliminated. On the other hand, those synapses that have been activated by *repeated early experiences* tend to become permanent. Experts like neurophysiologist Carla Hannaford tell us that physical activity and play during early childhood have a vital role in the sensory and physiological stimulation that results in more synapses.

In infancy, you can literally *see* the relationship between a baby's motor development and the resultant learning. As a baby moves from lying down to sitting to creeping and, finally, to standing, her perspective changes, as do her perceptions of the world and its possibilities.

The more mobile she becomes, the more she increases her knowledge about herself and the people and things around her, acquiring information through her tactile (touch), kinesthetic (muscular), proprioceptive (body awareness), and vestibular (motion awareness, or balance) senses. With each new experience, new neural connections are made. Still, there's some evidence that babies today are not physically interacting with their world as much as they once did. Not long ago, a pediatrician appearing on *Good Morning America* claimed that infants are spending upward of sixty waking hours a week "containerized" in such things as high chairs, car seats, and carriers. The National Association for Sport and Physical Education recommends that infants not be placed in settings that restrict movement for prolonged periods of time. But a baby today is likely to be fed in the morning (in a high chair), dressed, and carried to a car, where she's placed in a car seat. She's then carried into a child-care center, where she may spend much of her time in a crib or playpen. At the end of the day, when she's picked up, she's again placed in the car seat and carried back into the house, where she's fed, bathed, and put to bed. Even when parents and baby are home, there are too often activities that take precedence over getting on the floor and playing. With today's emphasis on being productive, simply playing with a baby seems almost a guilty pleasure.

All of this means fewer opportunities for babies to strengthen their muscles—to lift and turn their heads, to push up on their arms, to develop optimal balance, stability, and motor skills. It means fewer opportunities for the cross-lateral (right arm/left leg, left arm/right leg) experience gained from crawling and creeping. And because cross-lateral movement activates both hemispheres of the brain and stimulates communication between the two, too much time being containerized affects much more than motor development; it also impacts brain development and can later result in problems with reading and writing.

When a child's natural desire to move is thwarted, upper torso strength, rotation of the head, visual tracking, motor development, and other physical skills become much more difficult to achieve, and in extreme cases, require intervention from such professionals as physical and occupational therapists.

Early Learning Should Be Active and Authentic

Unfortunately, these days being containerized doesn't end with infancy. As I travel the country, I see (and hear from more and more early childhood professionals) that even four- and five-year-olds are being pushed in strollers or carried from the car to the school's door— all to accommodate hurried schedules. And, of course, there's all that time spent sitting with learning materials.

Certainly, it's easy to be convinced that flashcards, videos, and computer programs are contributing to an enriched environment and helping children learn. After all, we can see and hear that children recognize the letters or the geometric shapes when they pop up in front of them. They can say their ABCs and count to fifty—in two languages. But this and similar feats represent *rote* learning—the result of sheer memorization. *Authentic* learning involves comprehension. And until the child is developmentally ready to understand what the numbers, letters, or words represent—until the information has some relevance to her life—there'll be no comprehension.

Some rote learning has its place, of course; it's how most of us learned

PLAY & LEARN ACTIVITIES
Tummy Time

To give your baby a running start, be sure he has adequate tummy time. Acclimate him to this position as early in life as possible. Two to three times a day, after a nap or diaper change, place him on his tummy for a brief play period. You can gradually increase the length of these periods as your baby becomes used to them. Also, whenever possible, lie on your back and place your baby facedown on your chest. This not only helps him adapt to being on his tummy; it will also give him a reason to lift his head: to look at you! If your baby fusses while facedown, place a pillow, boppy, or other soft support under his chest, with his arms in front of him. Or lay him across your lap, raising one of your legs to create a slight incline. This will make it easier for him to see what's going on around him and should stop the fussing. Then, as he develops upper body strength, he'll no longer need the lift.

the multiplication tables and the state capitals. However, unless your child is going to grow up to become a contestant on television game shows, memorizing facts will have little use in life once he's passed all the tests schools require of him. Authentic learning, on the other hand—the process of exploration and discovery, of acquiring knowledge, of knowing *how* to acquire it (no one can memorize *all* the facts!)—will serve him endlessly. Moreover, authentic learning is far more likely than rote learning to foster a lifelong love of the learning process.

★

Crossing the Midline

To encourage crawling and creeping, get on the floor a few feet away from your child and encourage him to come to you. You can also place a favorite toy or object just out of his reach and encourage him to go get it—or place objects in a circle around him, to provide practice with turning in different directions. Crawl alongside him, "racing" or pretending to be a kitty or doggy. A favorite stuffed animal can also "crawl" along beside him.

Cross-lateral movement helps older children, too, so don't hesitate to pretend to be animals or have crawling races with your preschooler or primary-grade child. Walking, marching, and skipping also provide cross-lateral experience.

In decades past, children played with blocks, jigsaw puzzles, fire trucks, and other children. They finger painted and cut out paper dolls. They dug in the sand and splashed in mud puddles. They collected rocks and leaves. They made up games and rules and changed them when necessary. They touched, tasted, smelled, listened, and observed. They experienced! And because young children are concrete (not abstract) thinkers, who acquire information through their senses and by *doing,* they not only experienced; they also learned—a lot.

Today, time spent with "educational" products is replacing these active, sensory experiences with passive experiences. Children watch a DVD or verbally respond to the flip of a flashcard. They may have control of the computer mouse, but the software manufacturers have determined what they should see and hear. Screen time, computers, videos, and flashcards, in other words, don't engage children in the way that simple, everyday activities can.

When your child bangs on pots and pans, she learns more about cause and effect than she ever could by clicking on the limited choices offered by computer programs. She's also experimenting with sound and the force of her muscles. She learns more from manipulating blocks and puzzle pieces than from manipulating images on a screen—because she can't *feel* the images on the screen. Cutting, pasting, and scribbling provide more fine motor coordination, which she'll later need for writing and keyboarding, than does clicking a computer mouse. Helping you set the table or pouring water or sand from one container to another teaches more mathematics concepts than out-of-context numbers on a screen. The sights, sounds, textures, and smells of the outdoors offer more lessons in scientific principles than any two-dimensional media possibly could.

Are activities like splashing in mud puddles and cutting out paper dolls old-fashioned? Absolutely. Simple? You bet. But years of play research, as well as recent brain research, have determined that these simple actions of play and three-dimensional, sensory experiences provide the *very best* way for kids to learn. Can something as old-fashioned and simple as play really provide enough stimulation?

Without a doubt. In fact, what research has actually determined is that nature had it right all along: children, as with other baby animals, learn best through their play, movement, and tactile experiences—and learning in three dimensions trumps learning in two.

Active Learning Builds Language and Comprehension

"I was really worried because my two-and-a-half-year-old wasn't talking yet. Like the books recommended, I'd been talking and talking and talking to him, so I thought there was something seriously wrong. Then one day he just opened his mouth and was speaking in sentences!"

(Anna, mother of a three-year-old)

When we simply consider language development, we can see the value of active, experiential learning. It's no coincidence that baby's first word is a highly anticipated event that, once uttered, is captured forever in your mind and heart. You instinctively know that it's the initial step in an important, lifelong journey—and that language, both imparted and received, is vital to communication.

REALITY CHECK ✓

Researchers at fourteen universities have discovered a major link between children's language interactions with adults and their intelligence, academic success, and emotional stability. But according to TV-Free America, children spend an average of 1,680 minutes per week watching TV and only *3 ½* minutes per week in meaningful conversation with their parents.

But how do babies learn language? From where does that first word originate? It's not from exposure to flashcards, videos, or computer software, regardless of what their promotional efforts contend. No, children learn to communicate by *communicating*—nature has conveniently created us to develop language through interaction with others.

When you talk in that special way you do with your baby—when you sing him songs, read him nursery rhymes and stories—he wants to hear you, so he actively listens. That's not necessarily so with the characters on his computer or television screen. And since listening is a learned skill and essential to the other three language arts—speaking, reading, and writing—that first stage is critical. According to Jane Healy, author of *Endangered Minds:* "Children with poor auditory skills . . . have a difficult time learning to read, spelling, accurately remembering what they read long enough to understand it, or retaining the internal sound of a sentence they want to write down."

When your child physically moves over, under, around, through, beside, and near objects and others, she better comprehends prepositions—those little words so essential to language and life. When your child performs a "slow walk" or skips "lightly," adjectives and adverbs become much more than abstract concepts. When she's given the opportunity to physically demonstrate such action words as *stomp, pounce, stalk,* or *slither*—or descriptive words like *smooth, strong, gentle,* or *enormous*—word comprehension is immediate and long lasting. The words are in *context,* as opposed to being a mere collection of letters. This is what promotes emergent literacy and a love of language!

Similarly, if your child takes on high, low, wide, and narrow body shapes, he'll have a much greater understanding of these quantitative concepts—and opposites—than do children who are merely presented with the words and their definitions. If your child takes on the straight and curving lines of letters with his body or body parts, he'll be better prepared to replicate those letters on paper, and he will have acquired the directionality he needs to differentiate between a small *d* and a small *b*, for instance.

Along those same lines, if your child and her friends act out the lyrics to "Roll Over" ("There were five in the bed, and the little one said 'roll over' . . ."), they can *see* that five minus one leaves four. Similarly, the concept of magnetism will be much more fascinating to your child and her friends if they play with magnets—and then pretend to be them. The same fascination—and understanding—results when your child has personal experience with such scientific concepts as gravity, flotation, evaporation, balance and stability, and action and reaction.

Active Learning Builds Creativity and Problem-Solving Skills

When your child engages in fantasy or dramatic play, she's imagining "what if." This requires creativity. And although typically considered the domain of artists alone—and thus often considered expendable—creativity is a life skill, the ability to see beyond what

PLAY & LEARN ACTIVITIES
Sound Games

To promote active listening, play sound games with your child. With baby lying on her back, shake a rattle or other noise-producing object above her head or to her side, encouraging her to locate the sound. When she's crawling, hide behind various pieces of furniture, whispering her name until she finds you. Ask an older child to close her eyes and try to identify what's producing the sound you make. Then jingle car keys, clap your hands, cluck your tongue, or tap a drinking glass with a spoon. You can also take a listening walk, during which you identify all the different sounds you hear. For a greater challenge, bring a handheld tape recorder with you. See if you and your child can identify the sounds recorded once you're back home.

★

Use Language

Active learning equals optimal learning, and you can easily help promote this at home. When you playfully lift and lower your baby, if you

already exists, to imagine. And when one can imagine, one can envision possibilities and the solutions to problems.

True problem solving is the result of what's called *divergent production*—the ability to find multiple solutions to a single challenge. With software programs, children may be provided a menu of choices, but there'll be only one correct answer. In life, that's rarely the case.

Each of us solves hundreds of problems a day. It can be as simple as say the words *up* and *down,* she's absorbing the meaning of the words. For a toddler, preschooler, or early elementary child, create an obstacle course, inside or out in the yard, using empty boxes, plastic hoops, jump ropes, and pieces of furniture. As you and your child move through it, say aloud such words as *over, under, through,* and *around.*

★

Set the Table

When your young child helps set the table, counting out the number of napkins and forks contributes to mathematical knowledge.

★

Everyday Science Experiments

Give your child a paintbrush and a bucket of water and let him "paint" the outside of the house. He'll get some upper-torso exercise while simultaneously learning lessons about absorption and evaporation. Playing with bubbles or chiffon scarves teaches lessons in flotation and gravity.

producing a decent meal from leftovers, or figuring out where to look for the answer to a question, to the more complex dilemma of balancing a budget, or salvaging lost data from a crashed computer system. For some of us, problem solving involves getting along with difficult coworkers or family members. For others it involves launching a spaceship or ridding the world of cancer.

"Drill-and-practice" software, which involves the repetition of specific skills, no matter how it's disguised as game playing, doesn't foster creative thinking. One study reported in the *Atlantic Monthly* found that elementary school students using a favorite drill-and-skill software program for reading showed a 50 percent decline in their creativity scores! After seven months of working with this software, all of the students tested had trouble answering open-ended questions and were unable to brainstorm with the same level of creativity they had originally shown. There were no similar problems among children who were not using computers.

Imagine, if you will, a world in which people have lost the ability to imagine—to create. Of course, in such a world there would be no artists—no novels or movies to entertain us, no paintings to admire, and no songs to soothe our souls. But there would also be no new discoveries in science and medicine. No advances in technology. People would be unable to feel empathy, which is dependent upon being able to imagine what it's like to be someone or something else. And they would be unable to create solutions!

Now imagine what happens to a child's ability to imagine when she is surrounded by ready-made images and has no need to create her own. With the push of a button or the flip of her hand, she is presented with images the software programmers, video producers, and flashcard manufacturers deem important. Those images are *outside* of her head—absorbed through the eyes only—and not the result of an inner process that leads to the discovery of such concepts as:

- Flotation ("What happens when I put these things in the bathwater?")
- Balance ("How far can I lean in this direction?")

- Time and space ("What's the fastest way to get from here to there?")
- Color ("What if I mix the red and blue paint?")
- Sound ("What will I hear if I shake the oatmeal box?")
- Texture ("What will the clay feel like if I dunk it in water?")

These are all sensory experiences (and, yes, sensory deprivation is another consequence of a two-dimensional world, along with failure to understand cause and effect) that begin with an idea, proceed through a process of exploration, and result in a discovery. And it's wonderful when a child can take ownership of that discovery himself. Not only is the experience meaningful, but the lesson is learned and retained as well.

Early Learning Should Be Social and Stress-Free

A parent recently e-mailed me, worried about a new policy that was being implemented at her child's elementary school. It seems the powers that be had decided that before school began each day, the children would not be allowed to play and interact. Rather, they were to sit quietly and read. The idea was that this would promote the notion that school is a "learning environment," and it would help the children, once in their classrooms, to better focus.

The desire to improve our children's learning abilities isn't new. In the early nineteenth century, a minister, historian, and journalist named James Mills hypothesized that a man could rise to great intellectual heights if his mind were formed with that intention. So he set out to prove the theory by schooling his son himself.

PLAY & LEARN ACTIVITIES
Problem Solving: Movement Challenges

To promote your child's divergent problem-solving skills, present challenges that have more than one response. For example, invite him to discover two different ways to move on four body parts. (Possibilities include moving on hands and knees, hands and feet, or knees and elbows.) If he's walking the curb, the edge of the sandbox, or a low balance beam, invite him to find other ways to move along it in a forward direction. (Possibilities include tiptoeing, galloping, hopping, or scooting on the bottom or tummy.) Whenever there's more than one way to do something, gently urge your child to "find another way." With any kind of problem solving, it is the most

John Stuart Mills's education focused exclusively on the intellect. No attention was paid to his physical self. Nor was his social/emotional development considered; he was, in fact, kept from associating with other boys his age. But at three years old John Stuart was reading Greek from cards his father displayed. (Seem familiar?) By eight he was reading Latin, and by age twelve he had studied the works of Aristotle and Plato, among others.

And, yes, John Stuart Mills went on to achieve a great deal in his lifetime. However, he also suffered a nervous breakdown at age twenty and eventually came to realize that his father's relentless training had severely limited his capacity for emotion, the effect of which he struggled with for the rest of his life.

obvious solutions that first come to mind. A child will need encouragement to look beyond the obvious.

★

Problem Solving: Flotation

In the tub, give your child a variety of objects—some that will sink and some that will float—and ask her to discover which is which.

★

Problem Solving: Storytelling

Read a story and invite your child to make up his own ending. Or invent a story of your own, going back and forth between the two of you, one line at a time.

John Stuart Mills may have been the rare case of an overly pressured, emotionally troubled young person back in the 1800s, but today he would have plenty of company. Last year it was estimated that 15 million antidepressant prescriptions were written for children and teens. According to the federal Center for Mental Health Services, depression now affects as many as one in every thirty-three children and one in eight adolescents. One percent of preschoolers are said to suffer from clinical depression. Also, suicide rates among children ages five to fourteen have doubled over the last twenty years. Children may not be able to tell us verbally that they're stressed out, but they are showing us with symptoms. And other experts, including Joan Almon, David Elkind, Joe Frost, and Jane Healy, all point to increasing pressure on children and the demise of play in their lives as causes of these escalating mental health issues.

Of course, parents are hardly keeping their kids from associating with others their age. Nor am I suggesting that they deliberately set out to make an example of a child's intelligence or would intentionally deprive her of play. But if she's spending the majority of her time sitting at a computer, being tutored with flashcards, or otherwise being pushed to excel, she'll have little time for authentic play and social interaction. And that could contribute to some serious stress in her life—enough to have a long-lasting impact.

REALITY CHECK ✓

Research conducted at McGill University established that stress is associated with decreased learning and with memory and attention difficulties. In contrast, findings have shown that play reduces stress in children. Eric Jensen, author of *Learning with the Body in Mind*, tells us that "movement plays a key role in the release and reduction of tension." The conclusion? Relaxed, happy children learn more easily.

Furthermore, when a child sits in front of a computer or TV screen, even if she is in the company of others, there is little or no interaction taking place, meaning relationships are not being fostered. It also means fewer opportunities for speaking. As a result, a child may not as readily enunciate her words, formulate her thoughts, expand her vocabulary, or effectively express herself. As mentioned, our brains are wired to develop language through social contact.

On the other hand, when children play together, they learn to navigate the two-way street that is communication. Through play, they also learn to cooperate, take turns, share, resolve conflict, handle their emotions, and take another's perspective. Children aren't born with these abilities, any more than they're born with the ability to multiply and divide.

It takes a great deal more than academic "smarts" or raw intelligence to be successful. If personal and social awareness weren't necessary for success and happiness in life, only great test-takers would be triumphant. But the great test-takers don't usually end up as successful or as satisfied with their lives as those possessing great social and emotional skills—a topic we'll explore further in chapter 7.

Happily, research shows that creative play and movement activities—from make-believe to Follow the Leader—promote a wide variety of learning and social skills, all of which are necessary for success in school and in life. Although parents often consider word and number recognition the most important preparation for school, educators have found that social skills are far more critical to academic success. Education expert David Elkind concurs. In a 2003 article in the journal *Child Care Information Exchange,* Elkind cites the ability to work cooperatively with other children, take turns, and stand in line as among the skills necessary to success in formal schooling. Says Elkind: "If a child has these . . . social abilities, learning the academic skills is much easier than it is without them."

Early childhood professionals all around the country tell me that children "don't know how to play anymore." Patricia Stevens, a Head

PLAY & LEARN ACTIVITIES

Non-Elimination Simon Says and Cooperative Musical Chairs

When children gather at your home to play, instead of pitting them against one another in traditional games like Simon Says and Musical Chairs, teach them modified versions of these games that allow for continual participation and fun and success for everyone. With the traditional version of Simon Says, the children who most need to practice their listening skills and body-part identification are the first to be eliminated. To avoid this, arrange the children in two small circles rather than one large one. A child who moves

Start administrator, says, "The only thing they can do is replicate the actions of characters they've seen on TV, which is terribly limiting." Moreover, it does little or nothing to promote social/emotional or cognitive development.

Before there was so much competition from two-dimensional stimuli, when children had large chunks of free time—much of it outdoors—they instinctively played. Today that instinct requires some encouragement. So arrange those play dates for your child. Bring him to the local park or playground often, making sure he's in close proximity to other children. You can also encourage your child to play each day by:

- ensuring he has the time and opportunity to play
- limiting screen time
- playing with him. Not only will this give him someone to play with it also demonstrates that you consider play to be worthwhile. But

without Simon's "permission" simply moves to the other circle and continues playing.

In Cooperative Musical Chairs, the rules are the same, but the goal is different. You still take away one chair with every round, but instead of eliminating children who don't make it to the remaining chairs in time, the children are challenged to find a way to *share* the remaining chairs! In the midst of all the laughter, the children are learning to collaborate and solve problems. This simply modified game offers so much more than the fighting and hurt feelings that are part of the customary contest.

you must follow your child's lead! If you dictate the rules and direction of play, it won't technically be play for your little one.

Don't Forget

- Play promotes a wide variety of learning and skills, all of which are necessary for success in school and in life.
- Hurrying children's skills does more harm than good.
- By spending too much time in a two-dimensional world, your child will be deprived of authentic play and social interaction.
- Children are born with an inherent desire to learn and discover.
- Old-fashioned play and physical experiences offer the best opportunities for brain development.

2 ★ Ready or Not, Here Come Organized Sports

"My son was seven months old when I first felt the pressure to enroll him in programs. I had heard women I knew talking about the classes their kids were taking before, but it wasn't until that moment that I realized how competitive they all were. Here I was with an infant who had just learned to sit upright by himself, and someone was asking me what classes he was going to be taking, as if he were ten! When I told the woman that I hadn't thought about it yet, that I was going to wait awhile, she gave me a superior-sounding 'Ohhh.' I could tell she thought I was doing the wrong thing, that I just didn't know better. And maybe I'm reading too much into it, but it also seemed like she was secretly pleased, as if she thought here was at least one kid she wouldn't have to worry about competing with her son in school or on the playing fields."

—(Sue, mother of a one-year-old)

Karate. Ice-skating. Little League. Soccer. Gymnastics. Parents tell me all the time that they feel pressured to enroll their children in organized programs—particularly competitive, sports-related programs—often before their little ones are standing on their own two feet. Inevitably, they seem stunned by this unexpected source of anxiety, and they want to know why, in addition to everything else they have to worry about, they must also agonize over the possibility that they'll be failing their child if they don't succumb to the pressure.

It's interesting to note that the pressure parents are feeling is mostly coming from other parents—because these other parents have become convinced, somewhere along the line, that sports are serious business. They also fervently believe that unless they carefully supervise their children's skill development, their children won't live up to their potential—which would make them bad parents! Of course, the fact that their children's abilities are visible for all to see contributes to the high stakes: If their children don't succeed in sports, it's the parents' fault *and* evident to everyone else.

America has seen an astonishing escalation in competitive youth sports participation over the last two decades. During the period from 1981 to 1997 alone, there was nearly a 50 percent increase in enrollment. And though current figures are hard to come by, it's safe to assume there's been another growth spurt since then, as these days it's rare to find children who *aren't* enrolled in organized sports.

The reason for this phenomenon may be benign. As pedestrian- and play-friendly neighborhoods are disappearing, parents are more vigilant than ever, meaning children aren't as free to roam as they once did outside, unsupervised. And more parents are working outside the home, so they have to find something for their children to do in the afternoons.

But there are two other—perhaps greater—reasons for the youth sports craze. The first is that success in sports has come to be equated with success in life. To many parents, sports are seen as another avenue to a college scholarship, or even to an Olympic berth or life in the pros. Others simply look at sports as a way to make "winners" of their children, or to enhance the infamous college résumé.

The second reason is the pervasive notion that earlier is better, which is being applied to athletics as well as academics. Traditionally, youth sports were the domain of middle childhood and adolescence. Now we have children beginning their sports "careers" at three, four, and five years of age—and sometimes shortly after they've begun toddling (or stopped wobbling). For example, the American Youth Soccer Organization begins at five, but organizations like New Jersey Youth Soccer have "micro mini" leagues for kids as young as three, and communities in Long Island, New York, offer Soccer Tots for eighteen-month-olds.

Organized sports have replaced free play and unstructured time for even our youngest children. Instead of playing on their own, determining—and often making up—their own games, today's toddlers and preschoolers are being thrust into adult-initiated, adult-directed, adult games. Are organized activities the best alternative for toddlers and preschoolers? Will participation in sports lead to a college scholarship? Does success in sports translate into success in life? And if so, is getting started earlier really better?

Even if you believe the answer to all these questions is *no*, you may feel pressured to enroll your child nonetheless. After all, everyone else is doing it—and talking about it endlessly. What if, by chance, you're wrong? Could you be doing your child harm by denying him the opportunity to play preschool sports? What if he falls behind the other kids and never catches up?

In this chapter we'll look at the issue of readiness for sports and organized activities: what it means, why it matters, and how you can determine when your child will "have" it.

Why Readiness Matters

Would you consider handing *Hamlet* to your child once she had mastered her ABCs? Would you ask her to complete an algebraic equation because she had learned to count to ten? Of course not. And yet many parents don't think twice about enrolling their young children in organized sports for which their only preparation is the fact that they can walk and run (sort of).

Okay, so maybe T-ball and preschool soccer aren't the sports equivalents of Shakespeare, but the comparison still bears consideration. After all, a child who is asked to read at an adult level at age four is going to reach the assumptions—rather quickly—that reading is (a) too hard; (b) not fun; and (c) not something she can do. Her final assumption will be that reading isn't something she *wants* to do.

Similarly, when a child is placed in organized sports for which he is not developmentally ready—physically, socially, emotionally, or cognitively—he soon reaches the same assumptions about sports and, unfortunately, physical activity in general. The chances are then excellent that physical activity (*moving*, in whatever form it takes)—and its many health, social/emotional, and cognitive (yes, cognitive) benefits—will not be part of his adolescent and adult life.

It's true that participation in organized sports can offer children an opportunity for physical activity and social interaction—both of which are critical to your child's development. But when the requirements and expectations of organized sports go beyond a child's level of readiness and maturation, the experience will have more negative than positive results.

★ SUPERKID ALERT! ★

Myth: Where sports are concerned, starting earlier is better.

Reality: The positive aspects of sports participation can be negated when the experience demands more than a child is ready for.

Shannon, the mother of two children, told me: "I get some pressure because my kids aren't in any sports unless they want to be." Desire to participate, then, is certainly one sign of a child's readiness.

What else determines readiness? Well, it's important to remember that every child develops at his or her own pace. Still, there are certain "givens" where young children are concerned. One is that they're still growing. Their bones have not completely calcified, their muscles have not reached their peak volume, and their organs are not fully developed. Additionally, their bodies don't possess the mechanisms needed to relieve their bodies of heat; their visual perception is a long way from mature; and their eye-hand and eye-foot coordination won't be entirely developed for another several years!

In a nutshell, children are not just short adults. Among other things, expecting them to play adult games with adult rules and adult-sized equipment puts them in harm's way physically. Doctors, including fitness expert Kenneth Cooper, advise against high-impact sports like hockey and football for children under the age of eight because of the immaturity of their organs and skeletal structures. Soccer, which is thought to be safe for children of both genders, actually has a high rate of injury among young children. Even among professional players, almost one-third suffer at least one injury every season.

Where baseball and softball are concerned, the possibilities are even more frightening. These sports were recently determined to be the leading cause of sports-related eye injuries in children, with the highest incidence occurring in children between the ages of five and fourteen. Even scarier, during a seven-year period in the 1990s there were forty baseball- or softball-related deaths of children in that same age span. The primary causes of death were blows to the head, neck, and chest.

Among the reasons for these horrific statistics are the facts that:

- young pitchers can't yet throw accurately
- young children don't possess the reaction time needed to instantly evade a fast-approaching ball
- the chest walls of young children are thinner than those of teenagers and adults
- figure-ground perception—the ability to distinguish an object from its surroundings—doesn't reach maturity until eight to twelve years old
- depth perception—the ability to judge distance in relation to oneself—isn't usually mature until about age twelve

PLAY & LEARN ACTIVITY
Soda-Bottle Bowling

It's okay if kids' games aren't exactly the same as the adult versions. For instance, bowling might improve your child's eye-hand coordination, but it wouldn't make much sense to take him to a bowling alley and hand him a ball that weighs almost as much as he does. Instead, set up large, empty soda bottles in the backyard, hand him a beach ball or a big playground ball, and let him bowl to his heart's content!

REALITY CHECK ✔

Any games, sports-related or not, played with children should involve child-sized equipment or equipment made specifically with children in mind. For example, large foam footballs and big plastic bats should replace traditional footballs and bats.

According to the American College of Sports Medicine, more than three-quarters of a million children under the age of fourteen are treated in emergency rooms for sports-related injuries *each year*. It's frightening *and* ironic, considering that concern about children's safety is one of the reasons parents enroll them in organized sports.

Then, too, there's the potential for psychological harm. Though not as devastating as the possibility of physical injury or death, it is still very real and can also be life-altering. Many adults harbor continuing feelings of inadequacy resulting from early failures in sports and other physical activities. Since children have sports-related per-ceptions of their ability by *first grade,* we can see that these beliefs persist over quite a few years.

Finally, there is yet another reason why readiness matters: the very real possibility that children who are asked to perform tasks for which they're not ready will develop bad habits. For example, the child who doesn't yet know how to throw correctly isn't going to learn to throw correctly because he's pitching a couple of games a week. The child who runs with his feet pronated (feet rolling in with baby toes coming up off the ground) won't learn to run correctly simply by running. Rather, the chances are that these bad habits will become more ingrained over time, making it probable that the child will be unable to continue pitching or running.

But, you're thinking, *don't the coaches teach the children how to per-form these skills?* Unfortunately, the answer is *almost never.* Many well-meaning coaches, after all, are simply parent volunteers who don't know the correct mechanics of the motor skills involved. Other coaches are so intent on winning games that they focus exclusively on the skilled players, leaving the less-skilled kids to fend for themselves. Either way, it's almost always the game that matters—not fundamental skill development.

One of the great misconceptions about youth sports is the belief that children who are enrolled in organized programs are taught the skills needed to play—or to become physically capable people. More often than not, children are instead thrust into playing situations, given instructions that make little sense to them, and expected to go to it. It's rather like

---

★ SUPERKID ALERT! ★

Myth: Children who are enrolled in organized sports are taught the skills needed to play.

Reality: Children are more often expected to jump right in and play—with or without the necessary skills.

---

taking a child who can't yet walk and trying to teach him to skip first. These kinds of negative experiences can affect a child for years—if not a lifetime—whether we're talking about injury, perception of ability, or poor skill development. All of these possibilities are likely to produce a child who may have begun sports participation with the greatest of enthusiasm but soon is unable or unwilling to take part in any physical activity at all.

REALITY CHECK ✓

A study conducted by the National Youth Sports Coaches Association determined that *49 percent* of the five- to eight-year-olds surveyed were unable to perform even the most fundamental skills required in their sports. And according to a *Sports Illustrated for Kids* study, only 20 percent of youth coaches have had any training in how to teach necessary skills.

Building Confidence

For better or worse, our early physical experiences shape us. Most often, negative experiences and their resulting feelings keep us from participating in anything physical. Sometimes these feelings of inadequacy translate into other areas of life. On the other hand, feelings of *competence* can lead to success in areas beyond sports, as children who perceive themselves as competent tend to be more persistent after they've failed at a task. And, naturally, you want your child to possess both persistence and a higher perception of competence.

Fortunately, preschoolers are naturally blessed with these traits, as they're unable to differentiate between effort and ability. In other words, young children think that trying hard is the same as being able. That's part of the reason they're willing to keep working at a task, like throwing a ball at a too-tall basketball hoop, even when they are continually unsuccessful and long after an adult would've stopped trying. Still, there comes a point when even a preschooler decides it's not worth the effort. Unfortunately, she then also concludes that she's not good at this task—and believing you're not good at something feels bad. In fact, motivation theorists tells us that when failure is credited to lack of ability and ability is thought to be beyond control, the result is embarrassment, withdrawal, and a decline in performance. University of Chicago psychologist Mihaly Czikszentmihalyi, who gave us the theory of "flow," says people are happiest when the challenges they face are equal to the skills they possess.

The vast majority of parents believe that playing organized sports provides their children with self-esteem (a subject that's received much attention in recent years). But the opposite is more often true. Consider, for example, the likelihood of connecting foot to moving soccer ball, stick to puck, or bat to ball when, at age four, five, or even eight, eye-hand and eye-foot coordination are unreliable. When young children can't yet track objects, separate them from their surroundings, or judge their distance in relation to themselves (not to mention the fact that the sight of an oncoming ball often scares the heck out of them), how do they manage to catch, kick, or hit such objects?

When a child's ability to process information is still developing, he can hold only two or three items in working memory, and he may not fully understand the words the coach is using, errors are more often the case than successes. And when he's aware that his contributions to the team and winning the game matter quite a lot to the important adults in his life, he so wants to get it right.

For children to gain self-esteem and self-confidence playing sports, they're going to have to experience more success than failure (not in terms of games won but in terms of trying and succeeding, or at least improving). And when kids are under age eight, the odds are against that happening in organized sports. Then, not only is self-esteem affected, but the child's perception of her ability also falters, and she loses both motivation and interest in physical activity over time.

Developmental Traits of the Typical Preschooler

Young children have very specific capabilities and limitations-tasks they can and can't be expected to do at various stages of their development. This section explores the three developmental domains—physical, cognitive, and social/emotional—as they relate to sports readiness.

PLAY & LEARN ACTIVITY
Ensuring Success

To ensure your child feels good about his abilities, when you're playing or practicing a skill with him, scale back the challenge if he's not experiencing an 80 percent success rate. For example, if you're playing catch with a playground ball and your child drops it more often than he catches it, try a beach ball instead. If you're playing hopscotch and he can't yet balance on one foot, change the rules so he can jump (which uses a two-footed takeoff and landing) instead! You can try the playground ball and the hopping again at a later date.

We'll start with physical development—an area that we've already touched on and that is most often associated with athletics.

Physical Development

Children's eye-hand and eye-foot coordination aren't fully developed until the age of nine or ten. The ability to distinguish an object from its surroundings (figure-ground perception) fully matures between the ages of eight and twelve, and depth perception (judging distance in relation to oneself) isn't mature until about age twelve. All of these are related to visual abilities, and all have a tremendous impact on a child's sports participation.

Another aspect of physical development is peripheral vision, which refers to the ability to see things to the side while the eyes are focused on a central point. If you consider the need to be aware of other players in a team sport, as in soccer, or to avoid surrounding objects, like trees, when trying to catch an oncoming ball, you'll understand why peripheral vision is essential to sports performance. Then consider the fact that peripheral vision often doesn't mature until the teen years!

Similarly, although even infants are able to visually track objects that are moving slowly, it isn't until about age twelve that children can make fast and accurate judgments about quickly moving objects. In *Children and Youth in Sport*, Michigan State University professors John L. Haubenstricker and Vern Seefeldt illustrate the significance of visual

PLAY & LEARN ACTIVITY
Scarf Toss

Although you can't hurry your child's skills, you can provide opportunities for him to develop and practice them. To promote visual tracking skills, you might start by making a game of throwing and catching a brightly colored chiffon scarf. The scarf's color will help him see it more easily, and because it tends to float rather than fly, he'll have a greater chance to track it. Babies are likely to just watch the scarf—or to reach for it and miss. But they'll still enjoy the game. Toddlers may (unintentionally) catch it as often on their face or head as they do with their hands, but that's still fun for them. Preschoolers will love making a game of discovering how many different body parts (head, elbow, foot, knee) they can use to catch the scarf. Early-elementary-age children (kindergarten through grade three) like to find out how many times they can clap or turn around before the scarf reaches them.

tracking by using the example of an eight-year-old soccer goalie trying to intercept an approaching ball. They explain that she first has to locate the ball, which may require her to reposition her body. She must also quickly determine the ball's distance, speed, and angle of approach and predict where it will arrive and how long it will take to get there. Almost simultaneously, they say, "she must plan and then implement a movement response so that she gets to the intercept point on time and is positioned so that she can catch, kick, or deflect the ball to prevent it from crossing the goal line." If that seems ambitious for an eight-year-old, consider the possibilities for success when a four-year-old defends the net!

REALITY CHECK ✓

The typical child grows three inches and gains ten pounds between the ages of five and seven.

Beyond the visual realities is the fact that a child is still growing. This growth process includes muscles, joints, bones, and organs but also relates to body scale. Changes in the size of body parts in relation to one another can have a tremendous impact on strength, coordination, and balance. The size of a preschooler's head is reason enough for concern. It's the largest part of her body and, proportionally, has been likened to an adult having a head the size of a beach ball! It's a humorous image but probably not very funny to the frustrated four-year-old trying to keep her balance and coordinate her movements as she wields a bat, turns the corner at first base, or kicks at a fast-moving ball.

A child takes significant steps from the time he's an infant until he's a preschooler—literally, moving from a prone position to being upright and shortly after being able to run and jump. But it's a mistake to imagine the child can do any of these things *well*. Preschoolers are just learning to identify what and where their body parts are (by age seven, the majority know their large and small body parts), let alone how to use them. Using them in a coordinated fashion is simply asking too much.

Cognitive Development

An adult spectator at his child's T-ball game may find it enormously frustrating when an outfielder is picking dandelions when the ball finally comes his way; when the children on the bench discover a grasshopper in their midst; or when a multi-car train passing along nearby tracks, or a helicopter flying overhead, causes a major distraction in the middle of the game. But for kids such diversions are part of the magic of childhood. Young children have short attention spans because they're wired, at this age, to dabble—to have a wide variety of experiences. Children need to taste and touch and see and feel and hear all that interests them so they can discover which of these experiences appeal to them most.

Certainly as significant as physical development, then, is the issue of a child's cognitive development, beginning with her ability to pay attention. Children under the age of eight don't behave like "space cadets" because they're being unreasonable; their spaciness derives from the fact that their cognitive processes still have a long way to go, and it's perfectly normal for them to have an attention span that can be

PLAY & LEARN ACTIVITIES
Body Games

Body-part identification is an important first step in a child's physical education. It seems basic to us adults, but many a child has arrived in elementary school without knowing, for example, his elbows from his shoulders.

With an infant, to promote body-part identification, you can play a simple game of "I've got your nose (toes, fingers, etc.)!" With toddlers, you can play Heads, Bellies, Toes, in which you call out the names of these three body parts and your child touches the part being called out. Start off slowly, saying the parts in the same order each time.

measured in moments. What's unreasonable is expecting them to remain interested and attuned over the course of time it takes to get to a game, listen to detailed instructions (which their developmental stage doesn't allow them to completely understand), and play the game to its completion.

Still, it's not just the child's attention span (or lack thereof) that affects sports performance; a great many aspects of cognitive development come into play. For one, the ability to understand rules and strategies is simply beyond them; they don't have the capacity to comprehend the idea of tactics until they're about ten. That's why you can explain positions and passing until you're blue in the face and still get "beehive" or "clump" soccer. Or why your shouted instructions from the sidelines disappear in the wind—or, worse, cause your child to stop

Then, as he gains experience, vary the tempo and the order. A bit more challenging is Heads, Shoulders, Knees, and Toes, which is played in the same way as Heads, Bellies, Toes but with four body parts.

With a preschooler, you can play Show Me, in which you invite him to show you his various body parts, like nose, toes, fingers, knees, ears, and legs. Body parts that may be more challenging for him to identify include shoulders, elbows, wrists, hips, shins, and ankles. With this game, you and your little one can even trade off, taking turns issuing the invitations. For older children, a more difficult game involves inviting your child to place a shoulder on the floor, an elbow on a foot, or his nose to a knee, for example.

and wave at you from the playing field. Research shows that children don't even understand the competitive process until their middle to late elementary-school years.

Other cognitive elements involved are the facts that children need much more time to process information than an adult, or even an adolescent; and as mentioned earlier, they can hold only two or three items at a time in their working memory, as compared with the adolescent or adult, who can retain five to nine items. So if Coach is rattling off a list of instructions, there's little chance children will even be listening by the time he's finished!

Chances are also good they won't understand all the words rattled off anyway—because their language capacity is still limited. Not only do they know the meaning of fewer words, but young children are also quite literal in their interpretations. Darrell Burnett, author of *It's Just a Game!* describes two perfect examples of this: the child whose coach told him to "cover second base" and therefore threw his body over the bag, and the seven-year-old whose father told him to "mark his man" during the soccer game and therefore picked up some dirt and rubbed it on an opponent's shoulder! These humorous incidents are not rare exceptions, and they're certainly not intended to aggravate the adults for whom success in sports has become so critical. Rather, they're examples of kids being kids and why it's critical that we not have adult expectations of them.

Social/Emotional Development

As mentioned earlier, children don't understand the process of competition until at least fourth grade. Similarly, the "team" concept doesn't begin to develop until children are between the ages of nine and thirteen. That's partly because preschoolers are egocentric—which isn't obnoxious; it's just a stage of development. During the early years, children see the world as revolving around them.

Where sports are concerned, this egocentricity has two major implications. First, if children are going to be required to be part of a team, they're going to first have to learn to cooperate with others. But putting them in game situations that oblige them to interact in ways they don't understand is not going to teach them cooperative skills. After all, they're being asked to pass the soccer ball to teammates, to throw the baseball to the first baseman, and to hand off the football to the running back. They don't want to relinquish these precious objects, and they have no idea why they're being asked to do so.

Second, the fact of self-centeredness means she takes everything personally, including words that are meant as constructive criticism. Young children don't separate what they do from who they are. So if a coach or parent is telling them they've executed a skill incorrectly, they may take it to mean they personally have done something wrong. A child under the age of eight will feel as though she's being criticized *as a person*, so you'll have to be careful to offer kindness along with the critiques. (I'll provide suggestions for offering feedback in the next chapter.)

Remember, too, that anything that confuses a child is also likely to scare him. Imagine, for example, how terrifying it would be if, with no training in the electronics profession, you were suddenly thrust into the role of computer repair person. Someone deposits an implement in your hands, and your technical team is rapidly relaying instructions to you, most of which consist of terms you've never heard before. Moreover, there are people on the perimeter of the room shouting additional instructions and encouragement, letting you know how much they're counting on you. At this point, it would be pretty strange if you *weren't* in a cold sweat. But as an adult, you would have the capacity to put a stop to it—at the very least, to explain why you shouldn't be expected to do this. A child doesn't have that capacity.

Finally, if there's one common principle advocated by child development specialists and early childhood educators, it's that for young children, the importance of *process* far surpasses that of *product*. In art, that means the act of mixing and applying the colors teaches kids more than the "picture" that results. In early mathematics, stacking and restacking the blocks teaches vital lessons, whether or not

PLAY & LEARN ACTIVITIES
Cooperative Games

One of the best ways to teach your child cooperative skills is to play cooperative games with her. Here are a few of the simplest:

- Sit on the floor, facing your baby, legs straddled and holding hands. Gently lean back, causing the baby to lean forward. Return to an upright position. When your baby's old enough to understand, he can lean back, too, causing you to lean forward. Gently seesaw back and forth in this manner for as long as your baby stays interested.
- With your toddler, play Make a Face. Sit facing your child and begin by making a face, which she imitates. She then makes a face for you to imitate.

a tower is created. In early science, planting seeds and watering them matters more than whose flower grows the biggest.

In sports—or any physical activity, for that matter—the process is in the playing. Children don't care about winning, nor about how well they're playing—unless the important adults in their lives make it clear that *they* care about those things. What's important to children is that they have fun! They enjoy—and learn from—the *doing* and the social interaction involved in playing with others. For children, stopping in the middle of the field to chat with a friend counts more than scoring. There's more to be gained from the discovery of a garter

- With your preschooler, play the Mirror Game. Stand facing him and explain that you're going to pretend you're looking into a mirror and he's your reflection. That means he must imitate everything he sees you do! You then make simple movements—raising and lowering an arm, lifting a knee, or bending to the side—that he copies. When he expresses a desire to try leading, you can reflect his movements.
- With your early elementary child, you might play It Takes Two. In this game, you connect specific body parts (like right hands, left elbows, or backs) and discover how many ways you can move without breaking the connection.

snake—and in sharing that discovery with teammates—than there is from idly waiting for a ball to come your way. Counting the number of cars in a passing train teaches more—and is much more immediate (children live fully in the present moment)—than keeping score.

When Will My Child Be Ready for Competitive Sports?

"Sports were a huge part of our lives as kids. I played baseball and soccer and took swimming and dance lessons and also ran track and field. . . . To this day, when I'm frustrated and wor-

*ried, a long run cures me. . . . I'm excited about enrolling [my
son] in sports one day, but I want to be careful about how to do
it. I don't want him to feel pressured or pushed, and I know
there's a very delicate balance between encouragement and
overkill."*

(Kristin, blog posting)

Given their developmental skills, rare is the toddler or preschooler
who would be "ready" for organized sports. But there are exceptions.
And what about older children? Readiness is dependent on a great
many factors—that's partly what makes it so difficult to identify or to
prescribe specific ages. Readiness is determined by, among other
things, biological maturity, social maturity, emotional maturity, skill,
experience, the ability to understand and follow rules, and coordination. Other elements to consider include the physical and cognitive
demands of the particular sport and *parental* readiness (more on this
in chapter 6).

REALITY CHECK ✓

Children don't develop a desire to play sports for the sake of playing
sports until at least age thirteen. According to research, young children today are playing organized sports only because their parents
sign them up.

Unfortunately, there's no screening process to determine the readiness of young children for sports participation. Rather, programs are typically arranged by chronological age, a notoriously inefficient method of grouping children, as children develop at different times and different rates. Also, a program for, say, six-year-olds doesn't differentiate between children who've just barely turned six and those who are nearly seven. And in early childhood there can be significant maturational changes over a twelve-month period.

Moreover, the physical, social/emotional, and cognitive domains rarely develop at the same pace. Therefore, a child who has the body size and possesses the physical skills to play may well lack the social skills to cooperate with teammates or the emotional skills to handle loss. Similarly, a child who demonstrates advanced social and emotional maturity may be physically uncoordinated, or lack the strength, body size, or practice and experience necessary to successfully execute the physical skills required.

Stories like that of Tiger Woods, who started playing golf at age three and went on to become the world's greatest golfer, have led some people to the fervent conviction that a child who doesn't get the same early start will never have a chance. Nobody, it seems, stops to consider that perhaps Tiger was a rare exception. And there are certainly millions of stories—all of them unheard—of children who started before they were ready and quit out of frustration. Likewise, the stories of famous athletes who got considerably later starts hardly get a mention. Here, then, are a few of them:

- Greg Norman, one of professional golf's foremost money winners, never touched a golf club until he was sixteen.

- Karrie Webb, the world's number one woman golfer, started at age eight.
- In his sophomore year in high school, Michael Jordan was cut from the varsity squad.
- Cynthia Cooper, twice the most valuable player of the Women's National Basketball Association (WNBA), picked up a basketball for the first time at age sixteen.
- NBA all-star Hakeem Olajuwon started playing basketball in his late teens.
- Tom Brady, three-time Super Bowl–winning quarterback, had his first football experience in ninth grade—as a linebacker.

There's no scientific evidence that getting an early start leads to improved sports performance. There is, however, research showing that children who learn skills when they're *developmentally ready* learn them more easily. Furthermore, studies conducted with twins have demonstrated that even when one child is trained to perform a skill at an early age, in the end there's no difference in how the children perform. That is, one child may be taught to perform a skill earlier than another child does, but once the second child learns the skill, it's impossible to tell who learned it first. Parents must also consider the potential harm involved in trying to teach children skills before they're ready. First and foremost is the frustration factor. If something doesn't feel good to a child, she's not going to want to do it. And frustration feels lousy. Additionally, children who are "trained" by adults to develop at a pace that is not their own tend to become less autonomous people.

But perhaps the greatest disservice done to children who fail to perform ahead of nature's schedule—or are simply late bloomers—is that too often they are not given a chance to catch up. When children are categorized as "unskilled" or "untalented" in their early years, or when winning is what matters most and they're left to perfect the art of bench warming, this can affect their self-perception, leading them to choose not to pursue the sport involved. They then never get the opportunity to become skilled, or even talented, in the sport.

Making a determination about a child's athletic ability in early childhood is both premature and unfair. Many eight- to ten-year-old children are less skilled in sports than others their age. However, by the time they're adolescents or, sometimes, in their late teens, they catch up and not infrequently surpass the same kids who seemed so very far ahead of them. Michael Jordan and Tom Brady can probably attest that's true.

So in terms of your own child's readiness, bear in mind that the American Academy of Pediatrics recommends children not begin team sports before the age of six. Many movement experts believe age eight is more appropriate. But again, age is not necessarily an efficient guideline. Your eight-year-old could, for any number of reasons, be unprepared to participate. On the other hand, your five-year-old may be one of the exceptions.

When looking at your child with sports in mind, take into consideration his physical, emotional, and cognitive maturity:

- Is she coordinated?
- Is he as big as the other kids his age?

- Does she cooperate with others?
- Can he pay attention for minutes at a time?
- How well does she understand and follow directions?
- Has he expressed an interest in playing?
- And, once playing, does your child continue to have fun?

In the next chapter we'll explore what you can do to help your child get ready. In the meantime, resist the urge to enroll your child in a sports program just because everyone else seems to be doing it. Instead, make sure he has the time and space to *play*. Remind yourself that this is the only period during your child's life when he'll get to be a child. If you keep your expectations realistic, take your cues from your little one, and trust your instincts, everything will turn out fine.

Don't Forget

- Children are not small adults—physically, socially, emotionally, or cognitively.
- The positive aspects of sports participation can be negated when the experience demands more than children are developmentally ready to do.
- Every child develops at his or her own rate.
- Children enrolled in organized sports programs are seldom taught the skills needed to play.
- Chronological age is not an efficient way to group children, as developmental characteristics vary significantly among children of the same age.
- Sports readiness is determined by, among other factors, body size, coordination, emotional and social maturity, ability to take

direction, ability to focus on a task for longer than ten minutes, and the child's eagerness to play and subsequent enjoyment.

- Experts recommend children be at least six, or even eight, before starting in team sports.

3 ★ Helping Your Child Master Movement

> *"Watching the semi-finals of the World Cup soccer game—the agility those men displayed with their feet—all I could think was: 'They expect preschoolers to do this?'"*
>
> —(Rebecca, mother of a five-year-old)

Although we've touched on a few of them, this book isn't the place for a thorough, sociological exploration of the reasons why over the past couple of decades there has been a clear trend: parents have gone from letting their children out the door to play to controlling nearly every aspect of their children's movement experiences. But it *is* the place to reassure you that starting organized activities later does *not* constitute a disadvantage—and you won't be failing your child if you don't sign him up for sports and other extracurricular activities while he's still in diapers. In fact, you'll be doing your child a great service if you hold off until he's in elementary school, when he can make choices for himself.

REALITY CHECK ✓

The National Alliance for Youth Sports reports that 70 percent of children quit sports by the time they're thirteen years old.

In this chapter we'll look at movement experiences you can offer your child in lieu of organized programs—all of which will help to boost learning, prepare her to later be successful at physical activity in general and, should she choose, sports in particular. I'll describe the basics of movement and how your child can master them through a balance of play and practice, some of which you can help with. And I want to assure you that it's perfectly fine—and eminently human—for your child to approach a new task as a beginner and to follow a prescribed path in acquiring and refining that task.

It's Okay to Be a Beginner

Among the many consequences of the earlier-is-better myth is the perplexing belief that children must demonstrate mastery immediately. In the last chapter I outlined some of the pitfalls of labeling children's physical abilities too early, including the very real possibility that they'll never have a chance to discover their talents. But beyond that, just think of the pressure children must feel when they're expected to be superhuman. And it *would* be superhuman to master skills without going through the phases of learning, beginning with being a beginner!

REALITY CHECK ✓

There's usually a lag between knowing what to do and being able to do it.

Perhaps you can recall an experience of your own related to stumbling attempts to do something new, the gradual light dawning as it grew easier, and the eventual "a-ha" that came from getting it right. The experience that comes most readily to my mind involves country line dancing and the initial certainty that I was hopeless at it and destined to remain that way. It all began when my friend Patti and I decided line dancing would be a fun way to get some additional exercise. Patti and I were both physically fit and never imagined we couldn't handle it. After all, Patti was an accomplished horseback rider and a whiz on the softball field. And I had studied ballet, jazz, and modern dance at the college level. How difficult could it be to combine a slide to the right with a tap and a turn?

As you've probably guessed, it was a lot more challenging than either of us expected—because it was new and different from anything we'd done before. My most vivid recollection is of the two of us turning in opposite directions (*one* of us got it wrong) and crashing headlong into each other. Fortunately, we were old enough to realize we weren't alone in our dilemma. Still, despite the hilarity that ensued, there was that little core of wondering if something was seriously wrong with us—either mentally or motor-wise.

Over the course of a few lessons, things started to click. We began to feel comfortable with both the instructor's directions and the movements involved. Weeks passed, and we weren't stumbling around anymore. Eventually we were performing dances with multiple steps—and we couldn't believe those initial three-step routines had caused us such grief.

But that's the way it works with any new skill. Regardless of the person who is attempting to learn it (or of the age of the person), there will be an initial phase when the skill feels completely foreign and requires serious concentration. Gradually, your comfort level rises and less concentration is needed. Finally, you don't really think about the skill in order to use it in various contexts. Learning to skate is a good example of this process: at first it takes tremendous deliberation and effort just to remain upright. Eventually, standing on skates and then moving in a forward direction improve significantly. Finally, over a period of time, and with considerable practice, skating forward becomes somewhat automatic. But because skating backward and turning are new—and more demanding—skills, the phases of acquiring, refining, and (hopefully) mastering them begin again.

Physical education texts use different terms to describe these learning stages. One refers to them as *initial, intermediate,* and *automatic.* Another calls them *initial, elementary,* and *mature.* George Graham, Shirley Holt/Hale, and Melissa Parker, authors of *Children Moving: A Reflective Approach to Teaching Physical Education,* describe a four-stage process: precontrol (beginner), control (advanced beginner), utilization, and proficiency. And it's important to note that these physical education specialists assert that for most skills elementary-age students never reach the proficiency level—the stage at which a person is able to use a skill in changing environments and repeat it with increasing degrees of quality. (It is the proficiency level at which professional athletes perform. And believe me, they've worked long and hard to get there!)

Again, this process is not related to age (think *stages,* not *ages*). There are, however, other factors that contribute to the ease with which a person moves through the stages. At the top of this list of factors is applicable prior knowledge and ability. In college this knowledge and ability are often required in the form of a prior course known as a *prerequisite*. Where physical activity is concerned, the basics of movement serve as a prerequisite to sports.

Fundamentals First

It makes sense, of course, to acquire fundamental skills before trying to tackle the more complex ones. After all, you wouldn't try diving before you knew how to swim. If you were new to skiing, it would be a lot wiser to conquer the bunny slopes before heading to "Vertical Adventure!" The problem with many organized activities is that they inherently demand—rather than *teach*—greater movement skills than young kids have. Your son may well be in the position of having to catch a small white ball, when capturing a twelve-inch playground ball is still not a sure thing. Or your daughter might be expected to simultaneously run and kick before she can do either of those things well on its own. Such unrealistic goals can often lead to frustration and failure.

By focusing on the fundamentals first—by allowing your child to practice emerging skills through play, and by taking the time to play with him—you can help ensure that your child feels comfortable with and confident in his movement abilities. Then, should he venture into the arena of organized sports, he'll be much better prepared and much more likely to succeed.

★ SUPERKID ALERT! ★

Myth: The only way to ensure success in sport activities is to start playing sports early.

Reality: A child will derive far more benefit from first mastering the fundamentals of movement.

What are the fundamentals of movement? Listed below are the basic locomotor (traveling) skills. They're presented here in a general developmental order, from least to most challenging. You should be aware, though, that children acquire the ability to execute these skills according to their own internal timetables. That means, for example, that your child may well gallop before she jumps, despite the order presented in this list. Remember that every physical skill little kids acquire is a thrill for them. Even these basics are exciting. We may take running and jumping for granted now, but when we first discovered we could perform them, we couldn't get enough of them.

Crawl. The crawl involves lying on the stomach, with head and shoulders raised off the floor and the weight of the upper torso supported by the elbows. The accompanying locomotion involves moving the elbows and hips. Children should explore homolateral crawling (simultaneously moving the arm and leg on the same side of the body) as well as crawling with limbs in opposition (cross-lateral: left arm and right leg together, and the reverse).

Creep. This skill requires using the hands and knees or hands and feet to move the body through space. It is the child's first efficient form of locomotion. Children who haven't achieved a mature level of cross-pattern creeping should be given many opportunities to practice, even at ages four and five and older.

Walk. The walk moves the body through space by transferring weight from the ball and toes of one foot to the heel of the other. Continual contact is made with the floor. Limbs are used in opposition.

Infants begin to walk at about age one; by the time kids are age six, they have usually acquired a mature level of development. However, posture and foot alignment should be monitored. The body must be kept straight and toes pointed straight ahead, with the weight evenly distributed over all five toes. (Rolling in, with the small toes lifted off the ground, or pronation, is a common problem.)

Run. Running transfers the body's weight from the ball and toes of one foot to the ball and toes of the other. The body should be inclined slightly forward, and the arms should be slightly bent, swinging in opposition to the legs.

Running is actually one of the most demanding activities, requiring a lot from the heart, lungs, and muscles. For the young child it also makes demands on the nervous system, as all parts

PLAY & LEARN ACTIVITIES
Animal Games

Children love animals, so pretending to *be* a variety of animals offers a perfect opportunity to practice motor skills. Invite your child to gallop like a horse; jump like a rabbit or a kangaroo; walk like a gorilla, a turtle, or a duck; and run like a cat chasing a mouse. By framing your challenges this way, you help guarantee success. After all, your little one may not yet know how to gallop, but until he does, he can certainly pretend to be a horse!

of the body must be used alternately, symmetrically, and with perfect timing and an even rhythm. Balance while a person is running is more challenging than it is while walking, because the stride is so much longer and the tempo faster. Most children are able to run reasonably well by age five.

Jump. A jump propels the body upward from a takeoff on one or both feet. The toes, which are the last part of the foot to leave the ground (heel-ball-toe) are the first to reach it on landing, with landings occurring on both feet (toe-ball-heel). Knees should bend to absorb the shock of landing.

Leap. This skill is similar to a run, except the knee and ankle action is greater. The knee leads forward after the takeoff and is then extended as the foot reaches forward to land. The back leg extends to the rear while in the air, but once the front foot has landed, the rear leg swings forward into the next lift. Leaps are

★
Locomotor Fun

Playing "I'm gonna getcha!" or "Catch me if you can!" with your little one offers excellent practice with running, and even dodging. Trying to catch bubbles gives your child a chance to run and jump. Hopscotch provides practice with jumping and hopping, and Ring Around the Rosie helps with sliding. And once children have learned to skip, they'll practice it just it because it feels good!

often combined with running steps to achieve greater height and distance.

Gallop. The gallop is performed with an uneven rhythm. It is a combination of a walk and a run in which one foot leads and the other plays catch-up. Children will lead with the preferred (dominant) foot long before they feel comfortable leading with the other foot. Some young children learn this skill most easily when they can hear the gallop's rhythm—either with hand clapping, a drumbeat, recorded music, or sound effects.

Hop. A hop propels the body upward from a takeoff on one foot (heel-ball-toe). The landing is made on the same foot (toe-ball-heel). The free leg doesn't touch the ground. Children are able to hop at about age four. To maintain the balance necessary for successful hopping, they should lean slightly in the direction of the support (hopping) leg to shift the center of gravity.

Children should practice hopping on both the preferred and the nonpreferred foot.

Slide. This movement skill is a gallop performed sideward. One foot leads and the other plays catch-up, and the uneven rhythm remains the same as in the gallop. Because facing in one direction and moving in another is difficult for young children, they will learn to slide much later than they learn to gallop (usually not until they're at least five). Once learned, the slide should be practiced in both directions.

Skip. A combination of a step and a hop, the skip, like the gallop and the slide, also has an uneven rhythm. With more emphasis placed on the hop than the step, the overall effect is of a light, skimming motion during which the feet only momentarily leave the ground. The lead foot alternates. For many children, skipping initially on one side only is a normal developmental stage. Most children don't skip using alternate feet until they're about five and a half.

Also included among the basics of movement are *non*locomotor skills: movements performed in place, usually while standing, kneeling, sitting, or lying down. It's difficult to list them progressively, as many of these skills are acquired at approximately the same point in the child's development, but some are more challenging than others. The nonlocomotor skills are stretching, bending, sitting, shaking, turning, rocking and swaying, swinging, twisting, dodging, and falling.

Of course, depending on your child's age and stage of development, she can probably already perform most, if not all, of these locomotor and nonlocomotor skills. You may be wondering, then, why I'm putting such an emphasis on fundamentals. If your child can already do these things, isn't it time to move on—say, to sports?

Not exactly. Your child might be able to perform these basic skills, but it's highly unlikely he can perform them *well*—because maturation alone doesn't guarantee a child will reach a mature level for the performance of motor skills. As an example, an Australian study of twelve hundred students between the ages of five and twelve found, among other things, that the eleven-year-old boys were best able to execute a vertical jump, but only 11 percent of them could do it properly. Fewer than 10 percent of the children were able to run correctly!

The fact is, many children acquire the basic movement skills but only at the most rudimentary of levels. And without sufficient instruction and practice, they remain at those levels throughout their lives. That means they're unlikely to succeed in sports, or to be inclined toward lifelong physical activity. After all, a person doesn't typically get involved in activities he's not confident he can do well.

REALITY CHECK ✓

We can't expect children to perform like the professional athletes we watch on TV, who took *years* to master the fundamentals and progress through the stages of learning.

How, then, can you help ensure that your child moves beyond the basic movement levels? One of the most important steps you can take is to enroll your child in a preschool that includes movement education in its curriculum. If your child is in kindergarten or the primary grades, support the school's physical education program. And if there is no physical education program, clamor for one! (For more on choosing a school program, see chapter 5). But there are also things you can do at home, and we'll explore them later, in the section called "Playful Practice." First, however, I want to address the other two categories of movement skills.

Gymnastic Skills

In addition to locomotor and nonlocomotor skills, a third category of movement skills involves the "gymnastic" (body management) skills. Preschool and primary-grade children are capable of executing six of

PLAY & LEARN ACTIVITIES
Everyday Gymnastics

You don't need to enroll your child in a formal gymnastics program to help her learn body management skills. When she rolls across the lawn or down a hill, she's learning and practicing log rolls. When she walks the edge of the sandbox, or along a curb, it's just as challenging as walking a low balance beam—more so if the sandbox edge or curb is less than four inches wide. Climbing skills are achieved when your child makes her way up the ladder of the slide and later advances to trees. And monkey bars were made for offering practice with hanging and swinging! Don't forget: if you don't have these things in your backyard, you can always head to the nearest playground.

them: rolling, transferring weight, balancing, climbing, and hanging and swinging. These are self-explanatory, perhaps with the exception of transferring weight. In its simplest definition, it's the smooth shift of the body's weight from body part(s) to body part(s). Locomotion such as walking is considered weight transfer, because it moves the body's weight from foot to foot. However, transferring weight can also take place without locomotion, as when a person moves from a lying to a sitting position (simple weight transfer) or shifts the body's weight from the feet to the hands (advanced).

Manipulative Skills

Finally, there are the manipulative skills—gross motor skills in which an object is usually involved (manipulated). These include throwing, kicking, ball rolling, volleying, bouncing, catching, striking, and dribbling. Because these are the skills typically associated with sports, I'll describe them here.

Throwing. Throwing consists of moving an object away from the body, through the air, using the hands. After the infant-toddler phase of throwing small objects (food, bottles, etc.) in a downward direction (overhand), children generally progress from a two-hand underhand throw to a one-hand underhand throw to a one-hand overhand throw. Often, the size and weight of the ball dictate the type of throw.

Kicking. Kicking imparts force to an object (usually a ball) with the leg and foot (most often the side or top of the instep). This skill requires eye-foot coordination, body control and

PLAY & LEARN ACTIVITY
Ball at the Wall

With throwing, kicking, and ball rolling, children should be concerned with distance before accuracy. Invite your child to throw, kick, or roll a ball toward the outside wall of your house—at first while standing relatively close to it. Since the side of a house is a difficult target to miss, success is likely! As your child continues to experience success at this task, he or she can gradually move farther away from the "target." The next challenge is to try for accuracy—to roll, throw, or kick a ball through a plastic hoop held upright on the ground.

coordination, and accuracy of force and direction. Kicking for distance should be practiced frequently to develop a mature kicking pattern, while kicking for accuracy shouldn't be a concern until after the mature pattern has been mastered.

Ball Rolling. Like throwing, ball rolling involves moving a ball away from the body with the hands, but rather than through the air, the ball travels along the ground. Ball-rolling skills are most often associated with games like bowling and kickball but are also used in such activities as boccie, shuffleboard, and curling. The basic pattern is also seen in underhand throwing.

Volleying. For our purposes, volleying is defined as striking (imparting force to) an object in an upward direction with the hands or other body parts (excluding the feet). Typical body parts used for volleying include the head, arms, and knees, as can be seen in the game of soccer. Accurate visual tracking is necessary for this skill.

Bouncing. Bouncing, sometimes referred to as dribbling, signifies striking an object (most often a ball) in a downward direction with one or both hands. Motor development specialist David Gallahue tells us the developmental progression seems to be (1) bouncing and catching, (2) bouncing and ineffective slapping at the ball, (3) basic dribbling with the ball in control of the child, (4) basic dribbling with the child in control of the ball, and (5) controlled dribbling. (Again, we see those learning stages at work.) Although bouncing doesn't have much application later in life, it's an excellent tool for developing eye-hand coordination. The bigger the ball in the beginning, the better the chances for success.

Catching. The catching skill of receiving and controlling an object with the hands requires children to focus on the approaching object and make the adjustments necessary to receive it. Catching is often more difficult for some children who experience fear as the object approaches. Children will first catch with outstretched arms and later with the object trapped against the chest.

Striking. Striking, as it is used here, refers to imparting force to an object by using an implement (for example, a racket, paddle, or bat). This is one of the last skills children develop, because visual tracking is not refined until the upper elementary years and eye-hand coordination is more challenging at

PLAY & LEARN ACTIVITY
Pre-Soccer

If you think your child would eventually like to play soccer—or if you just want to have some fun that improves his eye-foot coordination—give him a beanbag, which is significantly less dynamic than a ball, to practice with. Once he's had considerable success with the beanbag, he can try controlling a small beach ball or a playground ball eight to twelve inches in diameter with the inside and outside of his feet. Once he's able to do this successfully (and remember, this process takes time, the amount of which will vary for every child), make a pathway (for instance, with two long jump ropes lying parallel on the ground)—and later an obstacle course—for him to dribble through.

greater distances from the body. The difficulty of striking increases with the length of the implement.

Dribbling. For our purposes, dribbling refers to the manipulation of a ball with the *feet,* as in soccer. Force is imparted to the ball horizontally along the ground, but unlike kicking (in which the ball can also travel in a vertical direction), the goal is not to impart force for distance. Rather, the ball is controlled by keeping it close to the feet. Dribbling requires eye-foot coordination, which is not fully established until age nine or ten, and a great deal of body control.

You'll notice that striking and dribbling are the two most challenging manipulative skills. (Yet every preschooler enrolled in soccer or T-ball is expected to be a pro at them!)

CATEGORIES OF MOVEMENT SKILLS

Locomotor Skills

Crawl

Creep

Walk

Run

Jump

Leap

Gallop

Hop

Slide

Skip

Manipulative Skills

Pull

Push

Lift

Strike

Throwing

Kicking

Ball rolling

Volleying

Bouncing

Catching

Striking

Dribbling

Nonlocomotor Skills

Stretch

Bend

Sit

Shake

Turn

Rock and sway

Twist

Dodge

Fall

Gymnastic Skills

Rolling

Transferring weight

Balancing

Climbing

Hanging and swinging

Just by virtue of involving an object, manipulative skills are more challenging than basic locomotor and nonlocomotor skills and therefore should be experienced later. Don't get me wrong, though: it's not my contention that you shouldn't roll a ball or play catch with your child until she's achieved total mastery of the locomotor and nonlocomotor skills. Ball rolling is a great eye-hand-coordination, cause-and-effect activity that you can even do with a baby. And what dad doesn't want to go out and throw the ball with his son or daughter? What I want to emphasize is that the manipulative (sport-related) skills are too often the sole focus of a child's movement experiences. And even then the child usually isn't taught how to perform them correctly; he's just expected to perform them!

Of course you can include manipulative and gymnastic skills in your play. But you should place the greatest emphasis on the basic motor skills—running, jumping, bending, stretching, and the like. Also, when first exploring manipulative skills, if you do it without an actual object, your child has plenty of opportunity to experience how these movements should *feel* without having to worry about correctly handling a ball, racquet, or other object. Finally, regardless of the category of movement skills being explored, you should never try to hurry your child's learning process, and you should build on the skills in a developmental order—that is, from least to most challenging.

Playful Practice

Perhaps, as a child, you occasionally walked the "tightrope" that was the curb, or swung on a tire hung from a limb. Other times you played games with friends or siblings—possibly tag and hide-and-seek. Or you invented games with made-up rules, games that involved maximum participation and maximum excitement. You ran for the sake of running, practiced log rolling down the lawn, and taught each other newly acquired skills, such as somersaults and cartwheels. Not only did you have fun, but the more you played, the more physically skilled you became.

In today's overscheduled society it seems we have forgotten that children can and do learn on their own, and they can do it through play. In fact, in early childhood they will become more skilled by simply playing on their own than by being involved in organized sports.

When I tell parents this, they're often doubtful, which is understandable. After all, we've progressed from one end of the spectrum to the other—from the days of carefree, unstructured play to carefully scheduling, organizing, and managing children's every game. If we hadn't experienced the former ourselves, we might not believe such a lifestyle ever existed—that children really managed without constant adult supervision.

But they did. *We* did. Some of us—those who especially enjoyed all that movement—decided to build on favorite skills and learn more. We took dance lessons or gymnastic classes or signed up for a particular sport. Some of us went on to become dancers, gymnasts, or athletes. Some took up skiing, bike riding, swimming, or golf as leisure activities. But almost all of us started out as kids just playing.

Sport psychologist Jay Coakley notes that when children get together and make up their own activities, they emphasize movement and excitement. When children play sports that are adult-organized and adult-controlled, the emphasis is on learning and following *rules*. Is it any wonder, then, that children acquire more physical skills when they are playing on their own? Coakley says he's "regularly amazed" by the physical skills children develop without adult coaching.

This isn't to say, of course, that you can't contribute to your child's physical development. You can. Surprisingly, the primary way is to make sure your child has the time and opportunity to play—alone and with friends or siblings.

A couple of years ago a young mom asked me if it was all right if her children sometimes played by themselves. I didn't quite understand her question and asked her to clarify. She felt guilty, she said, if she let them out to play in the backyard without accompanying them. She thought she should be *doing* something—playing with them, or perhaps just making sure *they* were doing something.

Having grown up as I did—with the idea of my mom accompanying my friends and me an appalling notion!—I was momentarily dumbfounded by her query. But she was so sincere, and I realized in the next moment that she wasn't alone in her concern; many of today's parents have been led to believe they must accompany, accommodate, and oversee their children at every possible moment. This young woman felt it wasn't enough to occasionally check on the children (as she perhaps took the opportunity to catch up on some housework). She believed she was failing them in some way if she wasn't right in the midst of their play.

Well, I'm here to promise you—as I promised her—that your children will do just fine playing without you. Actually they'll do better than fine—for all kinds of reasons. Among them is the fact that we want our children to grow up to be autonomous—independent, self-directed, self-sufficient—people! A child who hasn't had plenty of chances to be independent, self-directed, and self-sufficient isn't going to suddenly acquire such character traits as an adult. Nor is the adult who never learned to play as a child going to know how to keep himself entertained. Moreover, that adult won't be able to demonstrate playfulness to his own children.

Another reason it's important to let your child play on her own is the simple fact that, try as we might, we just don't think like kids anymore. We're not going to find the same things—for example, seeing how many hops it takes to get across the yard—interesting or fun. Such ideas wouldn't even occur to us!

So, yes, it's more than okay to just let your child play. And as he discovers how many hops it takes to get across the yard, how long he can stand on one foot, or whether or not he's faster than his sister or the family dog, he's acquiring, practicing, and refining his physical skills. And he's doing it in the best way possible for a child: he's having fun!

This doesn't mean, of course, that you can't occasionally join your child in play. You can and you should. Children learn much through imitation; they're genetically programmed for it. Joining your little one in play, therefore, serves a couple of important purposes: it allows you to model playfulness, and it allows you to model skills that your child has yet to learn, like a gallop or a skip. *But*— and here's the big qualification—it must honestly and truly be play. No expectations, no pressure. So if you demonstrate galloping or skipping, they should only be fun activities that you're encouraging your child to try. She doesn't have to do it if she doesn't want to, and if she wants to try, she doesn't have to get it right the first—or the second or third or fourth—time.

Here, then, are some other guidelines for playing with your child:

PLAY & LEARN ACTIVITIES
New Ways to Move

Use the elements of movement—space, shape, force, flow, time, and rhythm—to encourage your child to discover various ways to perform skills. (If we were to liken movement education to grammar, the skills would be the verbs—the *what* you're doing. The elements of movement, therefore, would be the adverbs—the *how* you're doing it.) For example, if your child were jumping around the backyard, you might ask her—playfully—to try jumping backward, sideward, or around in circles (the element of space), while being very big or very small (shape), as lightly or strongly as possible (force), with pauses in between (flow), slowly or quickly (time), or to the rhythm of your clapping hands (rhythm). Keeping the elements of movement in mind as you play with your child ensures that she'll get to experience the full range of possibilities for each movement. And that will be to her benefit in all future physical activities.

- Remember as much as you can about what it was like to be a kid. Think back to what you loved about playing, and you'll know what you want your own child to experience.
- Think *fun*. That's pretty much the definition of play. To practice walking isn't fun; to pretend to walk like giants and elves is. To practice running isn't fun, but fleeing from a pursuing mom or dad is!
- Think *variety*. There are reasons why children run wildly for a few minutes, stop to watch the progress of an ant in the sand, and in the next moment decide to slide down the slide. One is that

they tire—and recover—quickly, and these alternating rhythms allow them to keep going. Another—and perhaps the most important—reason is that they're interested in *so many* things. That's the way it's supposed to be.

- Allow your child to take the lead. It's not really play if someone else is dictating the content and pace. If it's not really play, it's not really fun. And for a kid, if it's not fun, it's not worth doing.

Providing Feedback

It's hard to watch a child—especially your own child—do something incorrectly and resist the urge to "fix" it. Often, our solution is to offer constructive criticism, a practice we see as both helpful and harmless. Unfortunately, what we say may be neither.

Young children possess two means of acquiring information about their abilities. The first is through exploration and discovery. A child sees someone else do a forward roll and becomes excited about the possibility that he could do it, too. So in the yard, in the living room, and wherever else he has the chance, he practices this move. The first couple of times, he can't get past the top of his head, so he eventually figures out he should tuck his chin to his chest. That helps, but once he does get over he ends up flat on his back, so he learns to make his whole body rounder. If he wants to do more than one in a row, he finally determines that if he bends his knees, keeps them bent, and finishes with his feet flat on the ground, it's much easier to launch into a second roll. That's self-feedback.

The second way children acquire information about themselves is through feedback from parents and other important adults in their lives. Such feedback is significant to them. They have a strong innate desire to feel competent *and* a compelling need to please the important adults in their lives. This makes for a powerful one-two punch and means we, as adults, have a responsibility to handle their feelings with care.

So the first thing to realize about constructive criticism is that to children it's just criticism. Furthermore, they don't always understand that our words are related to a behavior (their failure to bend their knees upon landing from a jump, for instance) and not to them as people. (Girls are particularly sensitive to what they hear.) Of course, if your child frequently lands her jumps with straight legs, or walks with her feet rolling in, or throws "like a girl," you're going to want to help her. And if the corrections appear to be something she can't discover on her own—through self-feedback—you *should* help her. You simply want to approach such assistance in the best way possible. Here are some suggestions:

- Make one correction at a time. Young children can't absorb multiple pieces of information.

- Use words you're sure your child can understand. "Go a little faster" makes a lot more sense to a preschooler than "Pick up the pace a bit."

- Correct the behavior, not the child. "See if you can try it with all of your toes touching the floor," as opposed to "You're walking wrong."

- A "sandwich" approach helps cushion the criticism. An example of this approach is: "That jump was really high. Make sure you bend your knees a lot when you come down. But you swung your arms to get really high with that jump." You'll notice that the constructive criticism is "sandwiched" between two positive remarks.

- Make your statements in the positive. For example, "Bend your knees a lot when you come down" is preferable to "Don't come down with straight legs." The reasoning has more to do with your child's developmental stage than with promoting self-esteem: young children often fail to hear the "don't" part of an instruction. In the example here, your child will most likely hear the "straight legs" part and do the opposite of what you suggested.

- When possible, use demonstration in combination with your words. The more senses used in the learning process, the more children retain. So if you demonstrate landing with bent knees as you explain it, your little one has a better chance of understanding what you mean.

- Don't compare your child with anyone else! This serves no purpose except to create alienation between your child and whoever you're comparing him to.

- Remember, you're also modeling *playfulness,* and in true play there are no mistakes. That doesn't imply mistakes aren't made. Rather, it means that if your child doesn't get something right the first time, she gets a "do-over"—but only if she wants one! (Remember do-overs—and how freeing they can be?) Most likely, she's going to want to accomplish whatever you've shown her, and she will try over and over again—sometimes while you're watching and sometimes when you're not. But she'll try because she wants to—not because someone insists she should. (You'll be relieved to know that in youth sports the most skilled players are typically those who initiate practice themselves and not those who are externally motivated by parents or coaches.)

- Use neutral, as opposed to judgmental, wording. Education experts say to avoid "moralizing" or judging when providing feedback. For example, a jump isn't "good" or "bad." A jump is either light or heavy, or high or low. If we use the former, we haven't told the child anything helpful. If we use the latter, however, we've provided both vocabulary for what the child did *and* useful specifics.

Finally, it's been said that coaches should use a four-to-one ratio of positive to negative remarks. That may be so, but I want to make it very clear that the phrase "positive remarks" does not mean praise, praise, false praise, and more praise.

Too many parents today operate under the mistaken notion that they can *give* their children self-esteem and that they can do so by constantly congratulating their little ones (a concept we'll explore further in chapter 7). Neither of these assumptions is correct. For one thing, *nobody* can confer self-esteem. (The "self" part of the word clearly signifies it must be earned by oneself.) And for another thing, even if self-esteem could be bestowed, constant praise—especially false praise—wouldn't be the way to guarantee it.

When I was teaching a college course in movement fundamentals, I brought in a group of local preschoolers for my students to work with on a weekly basis. And as they worked with the little guys, the phrase my students used more often than any other was "Good job!" I winced every time I heard it. First, it was both judgmental and nonspecific. What *about* the "job" was good? What information did these words give the children beyond the fact that the instructor was, for some reason, pleased? Second, when a child hears a phrase—particularly that one—over and over and over again, he stops listening to it. The words cease to have any meaning. Third, the praise was often false. The children *hadn't* done a good job but were nonetheless being told they had. And believe me, children know when something doesn't ring true.

So if you really want to help your child improve her physical skills, make sure praise is both deserved and specific. Together with your instructive feedback, your praise should provide information she can use to improve her skills. And *that* will improve her self-esteem.

In chapter 6 we'll cover what you should look for in an organized program, both before your child is ready to give sports a try and once he is.

Don't Forget

- Starting activities later is *not* a disadvantage.
- People proceed through stages of learning—beginning with being a beginner—as they acquire new skills.
- First mastering the fundamentals helps children later master the more complex movements involved in sports and other physical activities.
- Children can and do learn on their own, and they typically do it through play and self-feedback.
- In determining their abilities, young children also rely on feedback from the important adults in their lives. Your feedback should be positive but honest and specific.
- Remember what it was like to be a young child at play and you'll know what you want your own child to experience.

The Real Standards
for "Smart"

The bumper sticker reads: My child is an honor student at _____ School.

Parents have long counted on report cards to provide them with information about how their children are doing at school. A high grade in one subject meant they could relax where that content area was concerned. A low grade in another required extra vigilance with regard to homework.

Today, however, grades are seen as more than just a way to keep abreast of children's progress. If the grades are good enough, they can be bragged about from the bumpers of cars. And today's superkid culture has given rise to a special fondness for *labeling* children—"above average," "advanced," "gifted," or "honor student" among the possibilities. This penchant even has a name: "Lake Wobegon syndrome." In that fictional town created by radio personality Garrison Keillor, *all* of the children are above average.

But what do such labels mean? And what determines them? More and more often, in addition to school grades, standardized tests, which used to begin in the fourth grade but are now being foisted on younger and younger children, determine who's "average" and who's not—all in the name of accountability. The policy makers are convinced that more testing equals better education. As a result, parents are spending exorbitant sums of money hiring tutors and buying test preparation materials. They're holding their little ones out of kindergarten an extra year, whether or not they're developmentally ready, hoping that will ensure higher scores. And they're compelling their children to spend endless hours studying for endless rounds of testing.

In this chapter we'll consider the limitations of today's concept of a non-play-based early education and explore ways that you can help your child use her characteristics and skills to her best advantage.

How Your Child Is Smart

Especially during the early years, children must have the chance to explore on their own. Whether you're fostering what biology specifically endowed or awakening new interests, allowing your child to freely dabble in many pursuits—rather than specialize in one or two—will help her learn where her strengths and weaknesses, her likes and dislikes, and her passions and indifferences lie.

Helping your child utilize his own special strengths and skills may mean looking beyond what the policy makers and society typically consider "smart." Or as developmental psychologist Howard Gardner has put it, you shouldn't be trying to determine how smart your child is; rather, you should be trying to determine how your child is smart.

Gardner wrote an influential book called *Frames of Mind: The Theory of Multiple Intelligences.* In it, he contends that intelligence isn't a singular entity that can be measured only with paper and pencil. Rather, he says, we each possess many different *kinds* of intelligence, in various combinations and to varying degrees. To date, he has recognized nine different intelligences, all of which he's identified through a rigorous scientific process. For our purposes, though, the important point is that Gardner describes an intelligence as the "ability to find and solve problems and create products of value in one's own culture."

Although Gardner intended his work for the field of developmental psychology alone, an interesting phenomenon happened: educators pounced on the idea. Why? Because for generations they've witnessed multiple intelligences in the children with whom they've worked. Although our society most values the linguistic ("word-smart") and logical-mathematical ("number-smart"/reasoning) intelligences—the two intelligences measured by IQ and other standardized tests— teachers could see that many of their students had other gifts, other ways of "learning and knowing." Below, in no particular order, are brief descriptions of the intelligences Gardner has identified.

Linguistic. As indicated, people who are strong in linguistic intelligence are "word smart." As children, they may have demonstrated an early love of words, and they often grow up to be the poets, writers, disc jockeys, and public speakers in our society.

Logical/Mathematical. People who are strong in this intelligence are governed by reasoning. They are the scientists, mathematicians, engineers, computer programmers, and bookkeepers among us.

Visual/Spatial. People with a strong spatial intelligence understand how objects orient in space. They are able to visualize and have a strong sense of direction, design, and/or color. Career choices may include architect, artist, navigator, or interior decorator.

Naturalist. According to Gardner, this intelligence is built into the human nervous system and involves categorization and classification. It is the intelligence that determines sensitivity to one's environment. In natural surroundings, it allows people to recognize and discriminate among flora and fauna. In urban settings, someone with a well-developed naturalist intelligence would be adept at identifying such things as car models and sneaker brands.

Existentialist. People who question why they exist and what their role is in the world have a highly developed existentialist intelligence. The most recent intelligence to be identified by Gardner, it is closely related to the field of philosophy.

Interpersonal. Interpersonal intelligence allows us to understand and relate well to others. Psychologists, counselors, nurses, and child-care providers are examples of people who are strong in interpersonal intelligence.

Intrapersonal. People who are strong in this intelligence know themselves well—both their strengths and their weaknesses. They are usually self-reliant, independent, and goal-directed. Many entrepreneurs fall into this category.

Musical. A fascination with sound and with the patterns created by sound indicate a strong musical intelligence. Gardner believes this is the first intelligence to develop and that, if fostered, it can lead to a lifelong affinity with music.

Bodily/Kinesthetic. People who are strong in this intelligence solve problems or create with their bodies or body parts. Actors, dancers, and athletes possess strength in bodily/kinesthetic intelligence, as do surgeons and craftspeople.

It's important to remember that each of us possesses *all* of these intelligences but, as mentioned, to varying degrees and in different combinations. A surgeon, for example, has highly developed logical/mathematical and bodily/kinesthetic intelligences. The former incorporates the scientific aspect and the latter the meticulous use of the hands.

Where do your child's strengths lie? Does your son love to putter in the garden with you? He may be strong in the naturalist intelligence. Does your daughter create art everywhere, using everything from building blocks to mashed potatoes? Her greatest strength may lie in the visual/spatial intelligence. Is your child constantly dancing, indicating a developing bodily/kinesthetic intelligence, with some musical intelligence thrown into the mix?

When you're tuned in to your child's passions, skills, or intelligences—whatever we may call them—you can support their development and offer your child encouragement. Biology will certainly have

PLAY & LEARN ACTIVITY
Exploring Intelligences

There are a number of multiple-intelligences inventories on the Internet you can use to help determine your child's learning styles. (Do it for yourself, too; it's fun and informative.) Please note that these are *not* IQ-measurement tests, but assessments based on your child's preferences. Just type "multiple intelligences inventory" into your search engine. But remember, it's okay if your child isn't well developed in all, or even the majority, of them. I, for example, have never made a single checkmark in a list pertaining to the logical/mathematical intelligence. But I make enough checkmarks in the linguistic and bodily/kinesthetic intelligences that it doesn't worry me!

played a role in her interests and strengths, but the mainstream culture and the home culture are also influences. And since the mainstream culture—society and the school system—focuses on only two intelligences, you can help provide some balance in your child's life. This will be especially important if her strengths don't happen to lie within the linguistic or logical/mathematical intelligences.

As Gardner and his followers point out, it's difficult to identify special skills when we don't introduce young people to a variety of experiences. When the focus of schooling is on so few subjects, how is a child to discover passions that lie beyond such narrow boundaries? How is a child to unearth a love of landscape design, note a talent for composing, or cook up a desire to be a chef if his experiences have been limited to grammar, numbers, and technology?

One other point of which you should be aware: your child will use different intelligences for different tasks. For example, if she makes up a poem to help her remember historical dates, she's using her linguistic intelligence. If she makes up a song, she's using her musical intelligence. If you ask her to find a way to fit all of her toys back on their shelves, she'll have to call on her visual/spatial intelligence. And if she has to add by counting on her fingers, she's using her bodily/kinesthetic intelligence to get the job done. That's why it's important to give her a chance to further cultivate all of the intelligences. Opportunities to dabble and play can provide that chance.

At the preschool and elementary school ages, follow your child's lead, but don't get too invested in any one particular pastime. You certainly don't want to decide the rest of his life based on what you see in the earliest years. Children—and their interests and skills—evolve. And when he eventually discovers skills in *many* areas, as he's likely to do, he'll be able to make his own choices about his passions. That's why, whether we're talking about predominant intelligences, school grades, or the results of standardized tests, it's important to refrain from putting any labels on your little one. Instead, just know that the real standards for "smart" aren't found in school grades and test scores.

"Cookie Cutter" Curriculums

If you're the parent of more than one child, you know how different siblings can be. And when we imagine the myriad possibilities for genetic combinations, we can begin to imagine the differences among children in the same classroom. Throw in the various environmental factors, and it's impossible to envision the diversity in temperament, intellect, skills, and learning styles among a group of thirty students. Despite this diversity in children, in addition to the call for more testing (addressed later in the chapter), policy makers are now heralding the need for standardized curriculums: all teachers in the same grade teaching the exact material, with all students "learning" it in the exact same way.

What's Wrong with Standardized Curriculums?

We delight in the notion that no two snowflakes are alike. Yet "standardized" curriculums do not allow for the concept that no two *children* are alike.

There's nothing wrong with standards, or goals, per se. It makes sense to establish a certain level of mastery for children to achieve, and to determine what students should be able to do and know over the course of a particular period of time—a school year, for example. But the standards must be realistic. It should be possible for the majority of students to achieve them. That means the standards must also be developmentally appropriate—designed with the actual children in mind and enabling the children to reach them, each in her or his own way.

I believe individual teachers can best determine what goals are most realistic for a particular class of children. But often today's policies don't allow teachers to set the standards, or to choose or even modify the curriculum. Many states now require teachers—even at the kindergarten level—to follow a set *script*. For instance, according to a *New*

York Times article, all Chicago kindergarten teachers must use the identical curriculum, which not only dictates what they're to teach every day but also links every activity in the curriculum to a standardized test the children have to take. This means classroom after classroom following the same path from point A (digesting information) to point B (regurgitating it for the tests)—a scenario that typically entails the teacher's droning on at the front of the classroom, feeding facts into the children's heads and then handing out worksheets that give the children practice spitting them back out. What is the likelihood that kindergartners subjected to skill-and-drill are going to learn to love *anything*, let alone learning?

Another question plagues me: why do the powers that be ignore all the fabulous research we have available to us?

In *The Schools Our Children Deserve,* education specialist Alfie Kohn writes that he doesn't expect politicians to keep up with research in education any more than he expects them to keep up with research on kidney disease. The difference, he says, is that politicians aren't telling doctors when to prescribe dialysis, but they *are* telling educators how to do their jobs. Yet politicians are not the ones with the expertise in child development and educational theories. They haven't spent hundreds of hours in classroom or child-care settings, observing and working with young children. What gives them the right to tell the experts what to do? Both educators and research say that young children learn best through play, that actively acquiring knowledge is more effective than passive reception, and that children in the early years *are not ready* for academics (all of which we'll explore further in the next chapter).

Finland's Success Story

Other countries have figured this out. Finland, for example, allows children to learn through play until they're seven years old, at which time they begin formal schooling. Academically speaking, Finnish children do start off a bit behind seven-year-olds in other cultures, but they catch up very quickly. And then, despite the fact that they attend school for only five hours a day (compared with nearly seven hours a day in the States), they surpass their counterparts. Finland, in fact, ranks *first* in both reading and mathematics in the PISA (Program for International Student Assessment) tests given to fifteen-year-old students. The United States ranks fifteenth in reading and twenty-fourth in math.

Finland does have a core national curriculum that establishes the content areas and goals. But the teachers are free to meet those goals in whatever way they see fit—with or without textbooks, with children in small groups or large, indoors or out. No wonder the students are doing so well. And they enjoy learning so much that even teenagers list teaching as their favorite profession!

REALITY CHECK ✓

The United States spends more per student on education than Finland does ($8,287 per student in 2003–2004, according to the U.S. Census Bureau, compared with $5,000 per student in Finland), but with less successful results.

The Truth about Testing

Americans have an ever-increasing obsession with measuring and quantifying things. As evidence of this, consider that nowhere else in the world do standardized tests play such a large role in education. In fact, as of ten years ago, we were spending about *$200 million* a year on testing in the public schools (nearly double that of twenty years ago). I don't know why we're so crazy about test scores. Perhaps it began with the original IQ test, created in 1904, which was not actually designed to measure intelligence but to isolate mentally "defective" children who should be kept out of the classrooms. Despite this less-than-noble goal, the test became identified with intelligence, and the idea that one simple tool could pinpoint something as complex as a person's degree of intelligence took hold and grew to unimaginable proportions.

The original IQ test is still the model by which we judge a person's mental capabilities today. It has also spawned similar tests—today's standardized tests—that supposedly determine how well a child is doing in school and how well that school is doing in comparison with others. Between school, college, and the workplace, Americans take about *600 million* standardized tests a year. And all this despite what most educational experts, including Peter Sacks and Alfie Kohn, have to say: Standardized tests are indicative of neither intelligence nor potential.

Even so, increasing numbers of teachers across the country have told me they're now obligated to "teach to the test." In other words, rather than engaging students and drawing on the children's natural curiosity, teachers are now spending much of their time drilling students only on the facts and concepts that appear on standardized tests.

A Chicago-area mom told me her first-grade son's class is tested weekly on spelling and word recognition. A recent *Newsweek* article pointed out that "Kids . . . are tested, and tested again, to ensure they're making sufficient progress." Some children, according to the piece, are tested every ten days or so. One California school district tests students' reading and writing every eight weeks to ensure they're attaining school, district, and statewide benchmarks. In Boulder, Colorado, the district reading test is given three times a year. The mother of a five-year-old who had entered kindergarten excited about learning was understandably upset because regardless of how many times she was tested, her daughter couldn't read the required 130-word list. It wasn't the fact that her daughter couldn't master the words that troubled her; it was the fact that her daughter had become "exhausted and distraught" as a result of her school experiences—in kindergarten.

Problems with Testing

Experts assert that standardized testing makes little sense for children below fourth grade. Despite these arguments, the politicians and policy makers still pound podiums in their righteous insistence that "more testing" is what we need for accountability in classrooms. As a result, even preschoolers are expected to sit still and provide evidence of their knowledge.

The problem here is twofold: first, young children should not be expected to sit still for the length of time it takes to complete one of these tests. And, second, young children are very much still developing their communication skills. How can we expect them to fully communicate their *understanding* of something?

Moreover, we have to wonder how we can require children to communicate their understanding of that which is *beyond their power* to understand. Patricia Stevens, an early childhood administrator with a Head Start program in Midland, Texas, was the first to have to administer the new formal tests to the four-year-olds in Head Start. The tests, of course, were verbal rather than written, but this seemed to be the only concession made to the children's age. Not only were these little ones expected to be able to interpret graphs (a skill requiring highly developed logical/mathematical and visual/spatial intelligences), but they were also supposed to be able to describe a swamp. That would be challenging for anyone of any age (what *are* the right words to describe a swamp?), but it was especially challenging for these children, because they lived in *Midland, Texas*—a place so dry that swamps don't exist. How, then, were its youngest residents to describe something they likely had never come across in their lives?

Patricia has told me that these tests she's required to administer twice a year are so stressful that the children cry as they're taking place. They're so stressful, in fact, that she hires substitutes to give them, because she doesn't want the children to associate these awful experiences with their regular teachers. And Patricia's students aren't alone. The stress they undergo every fall and spring is representative of what is increasingly experienced by young children who are forced to endure standardized testing and curriculums.

As evidence, an Alliance for Childhood report cites mounting cases of school-related stress among young children, including more accounts of "kindergarten rage." Standardized testing has also given rise to increasing rates of "test anxiety" and, along with all the other stressors present in children's lives today, has caused the brains of many preschoolers to now resemble the brains of stressed adults, with excess levels of cortisol and adrenaline, the chemicals responsible for the body's fight-or-flight reaction. Children under stress are far less likely to do well on tests. In fact, brain research shows that high levels of stress impair learning.

REALITY CHECK ✓

A woman I know recently left her job as longtime principal of a New England high school. She had discovered the school's guidance counselor was manipulating the students' test scores to get them into college, but when she called attention to the issue, the public stood staunchly in support of the guidance counselor! *The principal* was the one who was vilified. Evidently, many students' parents didn't care *how* their children got into college, just as long as they did.

Although the claim is that standardized tests determine a person's potential—for later success in school/college and in life—their actual ability to do so has been "awful," according to Peter Sacks, author of *Standardized Minds: The High Price of America's Testing Culture and What We Can Do to Change It.* As one example, he points to the fact that women perform consistently worse on college entrance exams than men, yet women consistently surpass men in their actual performance in college. Sacks says the "poor ability of the exams to tell us much about later performance has been true both for people who score well on standardized tests and those who do not."

And what about the ability of standardized tests to measure intelligence?

★ SUPERKID ALERT! ★

Myth: Standardized tests are an accurate measurement of a child's intelligence.

Reality: There are many kinds of intelligence, and standardized tests fail to measure most of them.

Intelligence doesn't involve the mere accumulation of information. Intelligence involves knowing how to acquire information you don't yet possess and, most importantly, knowing how to *use* it once you've got it. In fact, there is a statistical link between high scores on standardized tests and what is considered "shallow" thinking. Too often, those who score well are simply good at memorizing or at guessing which multiple-choice answers should be marked. Standardized tests do not require the understanding, creative thinking, analysis, synthesis, or application of information that are the hallmarks of in-depth thinking.

In reality, we've been testing for decades in this country, and doing so hasn't done a thing to improve our children's education. But still we keep testing—to greater and greater extents. It reminds me of something I once read: that the definition of insanity is doing the same thing over and over again and expecting different results.

PLAY & LEARN ACTIVITIES
Promoting Individuality

Offer your child opportunities to express herself and to use her creativity. Play music of varying styles and invite her to move in whatever way she likes. Give her old clothes she can use to play dress-up. Invite her to tell *you* a bedtime story. Provide her with a variety of art materials and manipulatives (like building blocks and Legos) she can use to create. Most importantly, value *process* over product (the end result). If your child has painted a purple horse, don't tell her there's no such thing. Instead, validate her choice by positively saying, "I see you made your horse purple!"

★

Promoting Creative Thinking

Creative thinkers are said to possess "ideational fluency," which means they can produce numerous ideas. To promote creative thinking in your child, while you're doing chores or going for a walk or a drive together, make a game of trying to think of all the things that are round, for example. Or in what ways are a cat and dog alike? What things move on wheels? Don't make it a contest—just something fun to do that also happens to stimulate the mind.

The Myth of "One Right Answer"

A mother recently told me that her son had taken a standardized test in which one of the questions was: what are windows made

up of? Her son checked "glass" as the answer. Unfortunately, the
test makers considered windows to be made up of squares, so his
answer was scored as being incorrect.

I believe too much testing sends our children a message that there is only one right answer to challenges. Life just isn't like that. When a budget won't balance, there are many ways to make it do so. When a recipe calls for an ingredient you don't have, you can often figure out a substitution. When a customer is dissatisfied, there are usually various alternatives for rectifying the situation. When a conflict arises between people, there's no by-the-book way to resolve it.

REALITY CHECK ✓

"The world cares very little about what a man or woman knows; it is what a man or woman is able to do that counts."

—Booker T. Washington

In chapter 1 I described the value of process over product, and the importance of divergent thinking in creativity—not just in the arts but also in science, medicine, technology, and problem solving in general. But divergent thinking is not promoted in our school system. In fact, it is *convergent* thinking (solving problems that have a single correct solution) that standardized tests and curriculums promote.

Certainly, convergent thinking has its place in the world: two plus two will always equal four, and the right combination of hydrogen and oxygen will always produce water. But there is a real danger to our chil-

PLAY & LEARN ACTIVITY
Thinking Outside of the Box

Whenever possible, combat the "one-right-way" way of thinking by allowing your child options. If it's important to your child that she wears a purple shirt with green pants, take a deep breath and give her the okay. If you've given her a tricycle and she wants to sit on it backward and propel it with her feet on the ground, so be it. If she would rather lay her building blocks in a horizontal line instead of stacking them, it'll do more harm than good to insist she do it your way. It won't always be easy to remain silent while she makes choices that seem wrong—or at least odd—to you, but it will pay off in the long run!

dren if they grow up believing there is one right answer to *every* question or problem.

When children become convinced of the value of one right answer, what becomes of their critical thinking skills? How can they trust in their ability to solve problems? Business leaders, in fact, are already finding themselves among such people. One of their chief complaints about today's employees is their inability to think creatively and communicate.

Remember, positive standardized test results and high grades don't necessarily mean you've got a superkid on your hands, and negative results don't mean she's bound for a disappointing future! There are many definitions of "smart," and every child possesses skills and strengths. *You* know what your child's strengths are, and you're in a better position than anybody to help promote them. You're also in a better position than anyone to assure her that she's both smart and loved, regardless of her test scores or grades.

Don't Forget

- Standardized tests are not accurate indicators of either intelligence or potential.
- Standardized curriculums assume all children in the same grade are alike. From a developmental perspective, however, this is impossible.
- Standardized curriculums do not allow teachers to determine the appropriate goals for their students or choose the material to be learned. Standardized curriculums strip teachers of respect.
- Standardized tests and curriculums promote convergent thinking, but this stifles critical-thinking and creative problem-solving skills, which require divergent thinking.
- Children who spend thirteen-plus years in a school system that convinces them every question always has one correct response will be unable to work out even simple problems as they go through life.
- Standardized tests are developmentally inappropriate for young children.
- We each possess several different *kinds* of intelligence, to varying degrees and in various combinations.

5 ★ Is Your Child Playing Enough at School?

"If you get your child into the, quote, 'right' nursery school, it's a feeder school to get them into the 'right' kindergarten and the 'right' high school and the 'right' college."

—(A mom appearing on a *Dr. Phil* episode
about competitive parents)

Getting into the right school—*or else!*—seems to be the predominant line of thinking in today's superkid culture. As an *Atlantic Monthly* article called "Crying in the Kitchen over Princeton" pointed out, the common belief among parents (and eventually their children) is that "failure to gain admission to the Ivy League or to one of the nation's other top schools translates into second-class status for life."

Because no parent wants his child to be "second class," efforts to ensure a first-class education begin with gaining admission into an "elite" preschool—and that process can start with infancy, or even before. The *San Francisco Chronicle* told the story of one woman who called a popular preschool to say she was thinking about getting pregnant and wanted to put her baby-to-be on the school's waiting list. I learned about one mother who enrolled her four-month-old in "preschool prep." Others wait until their children are toddlers and then hire tutors. As one mom blogged, "Parents are getting tutors for their toddlers so that they can get ahead of the curve, well before the curve even exists."

These days it's common for parents to vie to enroll their children in what they believe are the best preschools. No hour is too early to line up, and no temperature too frigid, as exemplified by a 2004 piece in the *New York Times*. It described a "throng of 30-something, Type A zombies" (which included the article's author) assembled outside a prominent child-care center where they were eager to enroll their children. It was midwinter, and it was the night before the doors opened for registration. One mother had gotten there at 3:30 AM and one couple at midnight, but they were all preceded in line by the father who had arrived with his sleeping bag at 9:30 PM —during halftime of the Super Bowl. The author himself, although prepared for the twenty-three-degree temperature with ski clothing and a parka he had once worn for an Arctic expedition, wasn't prepared, at 3:50 in the morning, to be fifth in line.

Still, that story pales in comparison to one told on an ABC *Nightline* segment called "Preschool Wars." As reported, one mother was so determined that her daughter's application stand out that she wrote to the Vatican, asking them to write a letter of recommendation for the little girl.

These parents appear to be unaware that college admissions officers aren't remotely interested in a child's elementary school grades, let alone his performance in, or admission to, preschool. In fact, according to Gregg Easterbrook, author of another *Atlantic Monthly* article, this one called "Who Needs Harvard?" research shows that choice of *college* hardly matters. He cites research showing that kids who attended "moderately selective" schools went on to earn the same salaries in later years as those who attended Ivy League schools. He also points out that half of U.S. senators are graduates of public universities, only four of the top ten CEOs of Fortune 500 corporations went to elite schools, and that Steven Spielberg was rejected by two prestigious film schools, finally attending Cal State Long Beach.

Still, I understand the desire to provide a child with the best possible start in school (although I have to point out that education, particularly preschool, isn't going to be the sole determinant of a child's future). But what exactly constitutes the best possible start? Many parents are convinced it's early academics. Preschool directors and teachers all around the country tell me parents are putting increasing pressure on them to switch from play-based to academic-oriented curriculums. If the schools don't submit to the parents' wishes, they risk losing enrollment to those schools that do favor early academics.

Other parents consider the best schools those that "offer it all." For example, Brooklyn Friends, which is considered a prestigious private school, states on its Web site that their role is "to cultivate all of our children's gifts—verbal, mathematical, scientific, artistic, social, and kinesthetic."

Regardless of whether we're talking about preschool or the primary grades (and we'll talk about both in this chapter)—at whatever stage of life your child is—what's most important is that her experiences be "developmentally appropriate."

The National Association for the Education of Young Children (NAEYC) has determined, in great detail, what constitutes a developmentally appropriate early childhood education. Its leadership and members have written extensively on the subject. But for our purposes, the best explanation of what is meant by "developmentally appropriate" is a short list that appeared in *Child Care Information Exchange*. Written by Marjorie Kostelnik, the guidelines are as follows:

1. Developmentally appropriate means taking into account everything we know about how children develop and learn and matching that to the content and strategies planned for them in early childhood programs.

2. Developmentally appropriate means treating children as individuals, not as a cohort group.

3. Developmentally appropriate means treating children with respect—recognizing children's changing capabilities and having faith in their capacity to develop and learn.

In this chapter we'll look at what *really* matters in your child's preschool and primary-grade experiences. I want to help you evaluate your child's earliest education and advocate for the well-rounded education she deserves beyond that. And I hope that by the end of this chapter you'll no longer worry you're failing your child if you don't sleep on the sidewalks— or if her early life is filled with play rather than academics.

The Academics-Versus-Play Debate

As mentioned earlier, children are active, concrete, experiential learners, who acquire information and knowledge with all of their senses. Studies have shown that:

- Movement is the young child's preferred mode of learning.
- Lessons that are physically experienced have more immediate and longer-lasting impact.
- The integration of body systems allows for optimal learning to take place.
- The more senses used in the learning process, the more information retained.
- Play is linked to greater creativity and problem solving, improved reading levels, and higher IQ scores.
- There is a strong correlation between the time children are most playful and the time when the brain is making the most connections.

Given all of that, it seems pretty clear that there should be no debate: play is far more appropriate for a young child's first formal school experiences than academics. Yet despite this information, the educational efforts of such groups as NAEYC, and the fact that educators have for years emphasized the importance of educating the "whole child," preschoolers are now being required to do more and more seatwork. This includes producing worksheets that purport to show evidence of their learning, and following curriculums originally designated for kindergartners and even first-graders. (One mother wrote to me, complaining that when she picks up her daughter from preschool, she often learns that the class didn't get a chance to go to the playground that day because they "didn't have time.")

Why are schools devoted to making children simply sit still and learn? Part of the explanation comes from society's long-entrenched belief that the functions of the brain are more significant than the functions of the body. Moreover, we've labored for years under the misguided notion that the mind and body are separate entities. Thus, schools have insisted on training minds via the eyes and ears only.

REALITY CHECK ✓

Jean Piaget, a famous child development specialist who is studied in early childhood courses, explained: "Children have real understanding only of that which they invent themselves, and each time that we try to teach them too quickly, we keep them from reinventing it themselves."

In the past, based on what they knew of and observed in young children, early childhood teachers designed their programs to meet their students' developmental needs. Play and active learning were considered key tools to accommodate those needs and facilitate the children's education. Typical activities included:

- Sorting and stacking blocks and other manipulatives (mathematical knowledge).
- Singing and dancing, or acting out a story (emergent literacy).

- Growing plants from seeds, exploring the outdoors, and investigating at sand and water tables (science).
- Trying on various roles and interacting with one another at housekeeping and other dramatic-play centers (social studies).

Today, these types of lessons are steadily disappearing as the "earlier-is-better" syndrome takes hold, critically affecting the child's first experiences with formal education. Today, the curriculum once considered appropriate for first and second grades is being taught to children in kindergarten, and the kindergarten curriculum is foisted on children who are not yet five years old.

Even kindergarten through third-grade students should be doing less seatwork and more active learning, because, developmentally speaking, they're more like preschoolers than like their upper elementary counterparts. But instead of making active experiences a greater part of the primary-grade classrooms, we're instead making early education less developmentally appropriate for *everyone*, beginning in preschool.

REALITY CHECK ✓

Based on research showing that children who are developmentally ready have greater success in academics, a number of European countries are raising the age at which children enter formal schooling to six or seven.

However, recent brain research is confirming what many educators have believed all along: the mind and body are *not* separate entities. Eric Jensen, author of *Brain-Based Learning: The New Science of Teaching and Training,* confirms that not only do children learn by *doing*—and that movement is the child's preferred mode of learning—but also that physical activity activates the brain much more so than doing seatwork. While sitting increases fatigue and reduces concentration, movement feeds oxygen, water, and glucose to the brain, optimizing its performance. Moreover, learning by doing creates more neural networks in the brain and throughout the body, making the entire body a tool for learning. Active learning is also more enjoyable for young children.

Here's an example to help you envision the significance of active learning: a preschool teacher conducted a mock class with parents in

PLAY & LEARN ACTIVITY
Alphabet Fun

Singing the alphabet song helps children memorize the order of the letters. To help promote letter recognition, and therefore pre-reading and pre-writing, play a game in which you show your child a letter and then ask her to create its shape with her body or body parts. You can also create a large letter with a jump rope and invite your child to travel its shape by walking, tiptoeing, or hopping on it. Activities like these will help "imprint" the information on your child's body and in her mind.

which the lesson was to learn about kiwi fruit. Half of the parents were told about kiwis and then given a coloring sheet, along with brown and green crayons. The other half took a "field trip" to the tree in the hall, where they were able to smell, feel, and taste the fruit. Not surprisingly, the latter group of parents left with a much greater understanding of kiwis. (And these were adults who, unlike young children, were well beyond the stage of concrete thinking.)

Another example: several years ago I conducted a movement-and-music workshop attended by professors and students at a University of Maine campus, during which we moved to a song called "Robots and Astronauts." At the end of this workshop, two music majors came up to thank me because they finally understood the terms *staccato* (music punctuated with pauses) and *legato* (music in which the notes flow smoothly into one another). I was perplexed because these were, after all, music majors at the university level. How could they not have grasped these concepts before they attended my workshop? As it turns out, their professor had only given them the definitions for the terms. She certainly hadn't asked them to move like robots and astronauts, nor had she played them examples of staccato and legato! It wasn't until they had moved in punctuated and flowing ways, while simultaneously hearing music that was staccato and legato, respectively, that they really got it.

Eric Jensen labels the learning described above as *implicit*—like learning to ride a bike. At the other end of the continuum is *explicit* learning—like being told the capital of Peru. He asks, if you hadn't ridden a bike in five years, would you still be able to do it? And if you hadn't heard the capital of Peru for five years, would you still remember what it was? Explicit learning may get the facts across more quickly than learning through exploration and discovery, but the latter has far more relevance to children and stays with them longer.

REALITY CHECK ✓

Music educator Émile Jaques-Dalcroze once said, "I look upon joy as the most powerful of all mental stimuli." This is one of my favorite quotes—because it makes so much sense. Learning that is joyful creates a love of learning a child will have for a lifetime. Being a passive receptacle and required to perform in ways for which they're not developmentally ready creates children who have no idea how to use the information they've been given.

You don't have to worry that your child will fall behind if he is enrolled in a preschool that emphasizes play and discovery. Studies have determined that children who are enrolled in play-oriented preschools do *not* have a disadvantage over those who are enrolled in preschools focusing on early academics. One study, in fact, showed that there were neither short-term nor long-term advantages of early academics versus play, and that there were no distinguishable differences by first grade. The only difference was that the children who had experienced early academics were more anxious and less creative than their peers who had been in traditional, play-based preschools—a distinctive disadvantage. In another study, fourth-graders who had attended play-oriented preschools in which children often initiated their own activities had *better* academic performance than those who had attended academic-oriented preschools.

★ SUPERKID ALERT! ★

Myth: An early emphasis on "academics" will ensure a more successful future.

Reality: A young child is not developmentally ready for traditional academics and learns more through play and exploration than through "skill-and-drill" and worksheets.

Evaluating Your Child's Preschool

In brief, the preschool you choose should be one that respects children's intellectual, social/emotional, and physical needs. This describes a traditional, play-based preschool, as opposed to the academic-oriented education being touted—and sought after—in today's superkid climate. Obviously, then, when you visit preschools and interview teachers and directors, the word *play* should loom large at the top of your checklist.

How do you know what kind of play to look for? Among other things, a preschool in which play is a priority will include housekeeping, dress-up, and other dramatic-play centers that allow children to learn about themselves and the world around them. It will include materials, like blocks and Legos—enough to go around—for constructive play (activities in which children build or construct things). And it will be one in which the teachers play *with* the children! As I mentioned earlier in the book, many children come to preschool these days without having been encouraged to play, so early childhood teachers must be willing and able to show them how. They do this both by modeling and by asking questions that expand upon the children's ideas and encourage new ones. Although they follow the children's lead, they act as *facilitators* of their play and learning.

Of course, if the idea of a play-based preschool brings to mind a total lack of organization—children running wild, bouncing off the walls, and allowed to do anything and everything they please—you'll need to create a new mental picture. Play does not equal chaos or lack of structure; nor does an environment that is more child-centered than adult-directed. Rather, a preschool in which the children often initiate their own activities and make their own decisions will typically be more industrious than one in which children are forced to sit unnaturally still.

There are a number of reasons for this, including the fact that children who are involved in self-initiated activities have much longer attention spans than adults typically expect them to have. Because they love learning and are fascinated by so many things, when they are allowed to choose their own projects, their absorption is a joy to behold. Although this may be a source of puzzlement to parents who are accustomed to children flitting from one thing to another, it really shouldn't be: self-directed children are quite capable of losing themselves in what psychologist Mihaly Czikszentmihalyi calls a state of "flow."

Do the children experience music and art?
A preschool in which play is a priority will include plenty of music and art in the curriculum (more on the importance of the arts later in this

chapter). The children should have opportunities for group experiences, like singing and dancing together at "circle time" or collecting rocks and leaves on the playground for art projects. However, they should also have ample opportunity to explore these art forms on their own. That means there should be enough music and art materials readily available to and within reach of the children.

Music materials might include a variety of child-sized rhythm instruments, like tambourines, maracas, and hand drums. There should be child-friendly CD or cassette players, with headphones that allow for individual listening. And a child's wish list of musical materials often includes props with which to physically experience the music, like ribbon sticks and conductor's batons.

An art center should also include a variety of materials. Children should have the chance to express themselves with everything from crayons to clay to construction paper and glue. And once they are involved in a project, whenever possible they should be given ample time to satisfactorily complete it.

How much time do kids spend moving?

Movement, of course, should play a large role in the program. Teachers will not only use movement as a learning tool; they will also set aside time for both structured and unstructured physical activity. Guidelines created by the National Association for Sport and Physical Education (NASPE) recommend that toddlers spend at least thirty minutes a day, and preschoolers a minimum of sixty minutes a day, in structured physical activity. Both groups, they say, should also get at least sixty minutes of unstructured physical activity every day.

What's the difference between unstructured and structured activity? The former is child-initiated and unplanned. For example, on the playground some children may take advantage of the climbing equipment, while others slide down the slide and swing on the swings. Some children may ride tricycles, while others play tag or simply run around. Structured physical activity, in contrast, is planned by teachers (or parents), with specific goals in mind. Teaching children the correct way to perform motor skills such as jumping and hopping is an example of an appropriate goal. And because motor skills must be taught in early childhood, just as reading and writing skills are, it's not only an appropriate goal but also an important one. Whether or not your child ever plays sports, acquiring and refining motor skills will be critical to her overall development.

~ KEEP ACTIVITIES BALANCED ~

You can help ensure a balance between structured and unstructured physical activity outside of your child's school experiences, too. If he's enrolled in organized programs, like gymnastics or creative dance, he's getting the structured piece. Simply sending him outside to play should take care of the unstructured!

Is there social interaction?

Children learn a great deal from social interaction. Most parents know instinctively that socialization is a good thing. You don't want your child to be isolated, so you arrange play dates and enroll him in organized programs. You understand that only by interacting with others can he learn to be a part of society, and you want him to learn to appreciate and respect the company of others.

But even if she were playing with others on a daily basis prior to entering school, your child wouldn't have acquired enough personal and social awareness to last a lifetime. That's why preschools must foster development in this area—and kindergarten and elementary education must continue the process.

Social development is a long and continuous process. It begins with the child's own self-awareness and results, we hope, in his ability to interact with others. This process is likely to be stunted when children spend too much time confined to seats, bent over worksheets, and expected to function in their own little "bubbles." If education is about preparing children for the future, then that future includes functioning (and, hopefully, thriving) as members of families, the workplace, the community, and the world at large.

In *Emotional Intelligence: Why It Can Matter More Than IQ,* psychologist Daniel Goleman writes that he looks forward to the day when education includes the instilling of such "essential human competencies . . . as self-awareness, self-control, and empathy, and the arts of listening, resolving conflicts, and cooperation." He has a vision of what schools can do to "educate the whole student, bringing together mind and heart in the classroom." It may be too much to hope that such a thing could happen beyond the early years of a child's education. But it certainly can—and should—happen in preschool through third grade.

What's the noise level?

Given the importance of social interaction, a preschool environment should not be silent, or even quiet. A too-quiet environment would be one in which children weren't sharing their discoveries with one another and with the teachers. It would be one in which children weren't practicing their communication and other social skills. And it would be one in which teachers weren't asking children the questions necessary to extend their explorations and provoke deeper thought. The preschool you choose, therefore, should fall happily in between silence and "wall-bouncing."

Do children have nap time?

A preschool (or kindergarten) should validate the child's need for *sleep*. In too many programs today, the traditional nap time is disappearing as academics take greater precedence. As reported in a *Washington Post* article, the chief of Prince George's County schools recently told Maryland legislators that nap time had to be done away with. "We need to get rid of all the baby school stuff they used to do," he said.

REALITY CHECK ✓

Children from birth to age four require twelve to fifteen hours of sleep in a twenty-four-hour period.

But when, exactly, did children change? At what moment did their need for sleep—or at least quiet time—cease to exist? When did preschoolers suddenly stop being "babies?" They *are* still babies when we consider a typical lifespan. Young children—especially those enrolled in full-day preschools—need rest. Moreover, because relaxation is a learned skill, it is the responsibility of the adults in their lives to ensure that children have the time and opportunity to learn how to relax. Forcing preschoolers to power through their fatigue—as we adults must so often do—is not only irresponsible but cruel as well. So don't forget to ask about nap time in your interviews. And if a director tells you they've done away with that "baby stuff," let her know why you won't be sending your child to her school!

Is the school accredited?

Finally, NAEYC has established an accreditation system to help you identify good preschool and child-care programs. To earn NAEYC accreditation, programs must meet standards of quality that often go beyond state health and safety licensing requirements. They do, of course, recommend that the program you choose be licensed by the state. They also recommend child-to-teacher ratios of at least one adult for every five two-year-olds, for every seven three-year-olds, and for every ten four-year-olds. And they strongly suggest a program with trained staff, as research has found a correlation between the education of the staff and the quality of the program.

Questions to Ask

You can start your preschool search with a telephone interview. Ask the director about the qualifications of the staff, the rate of turnover, and the curriculum. Is it play-based? Does it include music, art, and both structured and unstructured physical activity? What about nap time? If you're satisfied with the answers, schedule a visit. It's in person that you can best observe the interaction between children and staff and the percentage of child-initiated activities. For more information on NAEYC's recommendations, visit www.naeyc.org.

★ SUPERKID ALERT! ★

Myth: The sole purpose of a child's education is to teach reading, writing, and 'rithmetic.

Reality: A true education addresses the whole child—mind, body, and spirit.

Evaluating Your Child's Elementary School

If you're planning to send your child to a private school, you likely have a choice as to which one it will be. If that's the case, you can look carefully at what each school has to offer. If your child will be entering public school, she'll probably be attending the one closest to home. You may not have a choice with regard to the school, but as a taxpayer and a concerned parent you do have a say regarding their offerings. If you find the school lacking in what you consider to be essential to your child's education, you can advocate for change. But first you need to better understand what's worth fighting for.

As I mentioned earlier, students in the primary grades are developmentally more like preschoolers than like kids in the upper elementary grades, so much of what I've suggested for preschoolers is also appropriate for early-elementary-age children. These children are still active learners who require movement, sensory experiences, and interpersonal relationships. Despite this, upon walking through the doors of the school, your child will be categorized along with all the children under that roof as an "elementary-school student." That too often means he'll be expected to sit still and learn.

However, throughout the school day, to meet their physical, social/emotional, and cognitive needs, children should have breaks from the rigors of traditional seatwork by way of the arts, physical education, and recess. In today's superkid culture, these three areas are increasingly considered frills and highly expendable as we strive to give students more academic—or computer—time. The truth, though, is that the loss of these three areas is influencing children in harmful ways, not the least of which is a negative impact on academics!

When evaluating your child's elementary school experiences, therefore, there are three essential questions you should ask. We'll explore them here, one at a time.

Are the arts included?

The performing and visual arts include art, drama, dance, and music. Educator Phyllis Gelineau, author of *Integrating the Arts across the Elementary School Curriculum,* cites twelve factors that the arts have the potential to promote. They are:

- sensory awareness
- verbal/nonverbal communication
- collaborative/cooperative skills

- imagination
- creative potential
- auditory/visual skills
- gross/fine motor skills
- cognitive, affective, kinesthetic, and aesthetic development
- sensitivity to diversity
- emotional release and stress reduction
- self-image
- self-discipline

All parents, it seems to me, would want most, if not all, of the above for their children—simply because of how these traits would improve their lives. According to Gelineau and other experts, these qualities also provide "a basis for enhanced learning." Research, in fact, has shown a link between exposure to the arts and academic success. In 1995, for example, a study determined that kids who had studied the arts for more than four years performed better on the SATs, scoring forty-four points higher on the math section and fifty-nine points higher on the verbal section.

As Gelineau succinctly points out, "Einstein's early musical experience and Galileo's visual art training may have been contributing factors to their later creative thinking." But what if exposure to the arts didn't have the potential to create future Einsteins and Galileos? Would it still be worth inclusion in the school curriculum? To my way of thinking it's a no-brainer. If we're going to educate the whole child, and thus create well-rounded people, exposure to the arts is a must. Sure, you can—and should—introduce your child to the arts at home.

Play & Learn Activities
Appreciating the Arts

Foster your child's art appreciation at home by paying attention to what interests her. If she's constantly dancing, make sure she has the time and the space in which to do so. Take her to live dance performances. Playing a wide variety of music in the house will not only inspire children to move in various ways; it will also promote an appreciation for this art form. Choose pieces in different styles (country, folk, jazz, and classical, for example), different textures (solo piano, orchestral, or voice alone), and belonging to different cultures (Native American, Irish, Latin, or African, to name a few). If your child demonstrates an interest in visual art, provide her with paints, clay, and crayons. If photos appeal to her, buy her an inexpensive camera, and encourage her to capture her experiences on film. And if it's drama she's drawn to, take her to live children's plays. Provide her with puppets so she can create a theater and plays of her own.

But children spend most of their waking hours at school, and it is at school that a wide variety of materials and teachers with specific expertise are available to them.

Unfortunately, the arts are not as valued in this country as they are in others. Being fluent in literacy, numeracy, and technology is seen as a way to make money, usually in business. Being fluent in the arts, on the other hand—or dabbling in them in order to have the occasional outlet for self-expression—doesn't typically lead to dollars. What worth, then, can it possibly have?

Well, if you have a love for a particular art—dance, drama, music, or visual arts—you're well aware of its value in your life. Although I once danced professionally (and I'm crazy about most forms of dance), it is the art form of music I can't imagine my life without. When I'm tired, music boosts my energy. When I'm down, music lifts my spirits. When I need a good cry, a sad piece of music provides a needed release every time. And what's a celebration or a holiday without music? Music has gotten me through some of the most difficult periods of my life and has been part of some of the most joyous. It has provided inspiration and motivation and company on a long ride home. On a daily basis, my life would be emptier without music in it. (The fact that it stimulates multiple areas of the brain is simply a bonus!)

If one of the arts offers you particular fulfillment, surely you want your child to have similar enriching experiences. By supporting the arts in schools, you can help ensure such experiences, while also ensuring arts educators don't have to spend so much of their time validating their worth and fighting for their cause. Having to do so is a sad waste of their energy. After all, even if the only benefit the arts had to offer was a heightened sense of aesthetics—greater awareness of the beauty around us—it would be worth inclusion in a child's life and education.

Do the children have physical education?

To every parent, school board member, administrator, or politician who ever had a negative experience in "gym class," physical education truly might seem expendable. Why spend hard-earned money on a subject they look back on with disdain? Why not just buy some more computers with the dollars saved from cutting the PE program?

Because we're talking about educating the whole child. Even if there were no childhood obesity crisis (which there is), and even if motor skills didn't matter (which they do), there's still the fact that the mind and body are not separate entities; they are interdependent and interrelated. Study after study has shown that children who are physically active have improved academic performance, higher test scores, and a better attitude toward school. In one Canadian study, for example, children who participated in five hours of vigorous physical activity a week had stronger academic performance in math, English, natural sciences, and French than did children with only two hours of physical activity a week. In France, students who spent eight hours a week in physical education showed better academic performance, greater independence, and more maturity than students with only forty minutes of PE per week.

Of course, it seems unfair to physical education specialists to only point out their contributions to academics. A healthy body matters, too! And unless you've been living without access to any media for the past few years, you've come across countless news stories about the childhood obesity crisis. Some of the reports you may have read or heard include the following:

- Overweight and obesity are growing at a faster rate among children than among adults.
- Heart disease risk factors, including hypertension and arteriosclerosis, are appearing in children as young as five.

- Children six to ten years old are dying of sudden cardiopulmonary arrest.
- Type 2 diabetes, formerly called *adult-onset* diabetes because it was almost exclusively an adult disease, is now so prevalent in children that the Centers for Disease Control (CDC) has determined American children born in 2000 face a one-in-three chance of developing it.
- Because of obesity, today's children may have life spans that are one to five years shorter than they otherwise would have been.
- For the first time in two centuries, today's children may not have as long a life span as their parents.

Inactive children tend to become inactive adults, and sedentary living is the primary cause of overweight and obesity. PE may once have been about dodge ball and field hockey, but today it's about promoting lifelong fitness. The PE specialist has the expertise to help children acquire and refine motor skills, ensuring they'll have the confidence to be physically active, and to teach children the principles of health-related fitness.

If we want our children to be healthy, to learn how to achieve and maintain fitness, and to be active for a lifetime, we'll speak up in favor of PE and help ensure it remains in—or is returned to—the elementary school curriculum.

Do the children have recess?

Did you know that many elementary schools—an estimated 40 percent—have eliminated recess from the daily schedule? And that some elementary schools are now being built without playgrounds? To those of us with fond memories of those highly anticipated, liberating periods, the thought is appalling. But it's not as appalling as the total dismissal of research demonstrating the importance of recess.

We've already reviewed the fact that physical activity in general contributes to the child's welfare in numerous ways. Here is some of what else we know:

- Prolonged confinement in classrooms results in restlessness and fidgeting.
- Children who are physically active in school are more likely to be physically active at home.
- The outside light stimulates the pineal gland, which is the part of the brain that helps regulate our biological clock, is vital to the immune system, and makes us feel happier.
- Outside light triggers the synthesis of vitamin D.
- A number of studies have demonstrated that outside light increases academic learning and productivity.

Even as far back as 1885 and 1901, research showed that people learn better and more quickly when their efforts are distributed (breaks are included) than when concentrated (work is conducted in longer periods), and when they have a change of pace. This is especially true of young children because of the immaturity of their nervous systems.

Again, the thought is that recess, like nap time, is a waste of time that could be better spent on academics. But research by Professor Olga Jarrett and her colleagues demonstrated that a fifteen-minute recess resulted in the children being 5 percent more on task and 9 percent less fidgety. Translation: a fifteen-minute recess saved *twenty* minutes during the day.

REALITY CHECK ✓

Research shows that the learning brain can pay attention to something for only about twenty minutes.

A colleague recently gave me a wonderful example of what it must be like for children to go all day without recess. She asks parents to recall a day spent at a conference or business meeting that required them to sit and listen all day long. Unlike a typical day, during which they're able to take breaks when needed—to get up and stretch or walk to the water cooler—when at a conference or in a meeting, people are usually required to sit in one seat, with as little fidgeting as possible, for hours at a stretch. Invariably, they're far more tired at the end of one of these days, but because they've done nothing but sit, they're mystified as to why they're so exhausted. The reason, according to Eric Jensen, is that sitting for more than ten minutes at a time "reduces our awareness of physical and emotional sensations and increases fatigue."

Because increased fatigue renders concentration difficult (if not impossible), doesn't it make more sense to provide children with breaks than to force them to remain in situations that can't possibly be productive? In Finland—a country, as you'll recall, that is number one in the world in literacy and numeracy—they've decided that regular breaks make a lot more sense. That's why all of their students, from first to ninth grade, have a fifteen-minute break after *every forty-five minutes of class work.* (Finnish students also take art, music, and physical education.)

REALITY CHECK ✓

A survey conducted by the National PTA found that *99 percent* of teachers and parents believe recess is important for elementary school students. That means these teachers and parents outnumber the policy makers who favor focusing on academics all day long! For research on the subjects of physical activity, physical education, and recess—or for suggestions on how you can advocate for them in your child's school—go to the Web sites of the American Association for the Child's Right to Play (www.ipausa.org) and the National Association for Sport and Physical Education (www.aahperd.org/naspe). Also, sponsored by the Cartoon Network, is www.rescuingrecess.com.

Do Computers Belong in the Classroom?

Generating considerable debate is the subject of computers in preschool and early elementary classrooms—or the importance of an early introduction to technology in general. On one side are those who believe there's no need to hurry children's skills, including technical skills. On the other side are those who believe that getting an early start with computers—similar to that promoted for academics and sports— is necessary if children are to gain a competitive edge, and they label reluctant teachers who prefer that students learn in more active ways as "dinosaurs" and "technophobes."

There's no question that technology has changed the way we live, particularly in the last decade. New technologies are provoking so much excitement in education that hundreds of thousands of dollars are being spent to ensure classrooms are "wired"—but this is often at the expense of the arts and physical education. Computer labs replace art and music rooms, meaning art and music teachers are being rendered expendable. And when it comes time to trim the budget, PE is considered more dispensable than computers every time.

Yes, technology is becoming increasingly more important in our lives. And, yes, regardless of the field your child enters computer literacy will probably be a must. But waiting to acquire computer literacy is unlikely to have a negative impact on your child's future. Children acquire computer skills very easily, even if they wait until elementary school or later. Take today's college graduates: twenty-two-year-old Michael, for example, used a computer for the first time in fifth or sixth grade (they simply weren't around before that). It wasn't until he was a sophomore in high school that he got one of his own. Still, despite this "late" start, he graduated from Rensselaer Polytechnic Institute in 2004 with a degree in mechanical engineering. He now has a position he loves, writing engineering software, and one of his hobbies is rebuilding computers from spare parts.

Experts, including Jane Healy, author of *Failure to Connect: How Computers Affect Our Children's Minds—and What We Can Do About It*, say there's no need for children to be exposed to computers before the age of seven. And it makes sense when we stop to consider what we know about child and brain development and how children learn. As we've already explored, children need to learn through their senses, through movement, and through social interaction. None of that is possible at the computer! Furthermore, putting children in front of computers in the preschool or early elementary classroom ensures *more* screen time in their lives. As Alison Armstrong and Charles Casement, authors of *The Child and the Machine: How Computers Put Our Children's Education at Risk,* point out, preschool was previously at least a place "that served as an antidote to an excess of electronic stimulation at home" and where children could get a variety of experiences they weren't likely to have anywhere else.

The Vision Impact

Also compelling is the impact that staring at a screen has on a young child's vision. At a recent educational conference, in a workshop on brain research I listened as teachers discussed what is worrying them most about today's children. At the top of the list is the fact that they (along with a number of doctors) are seeing more and more children with vision problems. They were flabbergasted at the number of kids losing not only the ability to shift their focus from near to far (and the reverse), but also the ability to move their eyes from left to right.

In a society where reading and writing occur from left to right, this is no small problem. The American Optometric Association tells us that children should be able to move their eyes easily across the page and to shift them quickly from one object to another. They further list as necessary for learning both near (ten to thirteen inches) and distance (beyond arm's reach) vision, the ability to change focus quickly, and peripheral vision.

All of these visual abilities are being lost, partly as a result of what neurophysiologist Carla Hannaford calls "ocular lock," which occurs when one sits motionless staring at a flat screen. Author of the book *Smart Moves: Why Learning Is Not All in Your Head,* Hannaford asserts that our eyes must be actively moving in order for learning to take place.

As you can imagine, the visual process is technical and complex. What you may not realize is that vision is dependent on integration with other body systems, including the sense of touch and *motor experience.* Hannaford tells us that less than 10 percent of the visual process occurs in the eyes, with the remaining 90 percent taking place "in the brain from association with touch and proprioception" (our sense of the body's position in space).

It is in three-dimensional environments like the outdoors, Hannaford says, that the eyes are "in constant motion gathering sensory information to build intricate image packages necessary for learning. The brain integrates these image packages with other sensory information like touch and proprioception to build a visual perception system. The eyes are equipped with different kinds of visual focus, of which three-dimensional focus is vital for learning, yet we emphasize two-dimensional focus in learning situations."

REALITY CHECK ✔

Schools aren't likely to shift gears and begin placing more emphasis on three-dimensional learning. But you can, and you should. Among other things, you can place restrictions on your child's screen time. The American Academy of Pediatrics recommends no screen time for children under two, and only one to two hours a day, including television viewing, for children three to five. If your child has spent an hour in front of a screen, insist that she turn it off and go play (preferably outside). When she doesn't have electronics to keep her amused, she'll find other ways to entertain herself, which will teach her considerably more than the computer can!

We need to seriously consider that because hours of computer time are a fairly recent part of children's lives, we can't yet know what all of the long-term consequences may be. It's not unexpected that there could be vision problems. Too much time at the computer also means children will have less movement in their lives! This will impact both their motor and cognitive development, and it could very well contribute to our troubles with childhood overweight and obesity (a subject tackled earlier in the chapter).

Would Michael's life be different if he had started with lapware or if he had gone to a preschool with computers available? We'll never know. I strongly believe, however, that Michael's success was far more a result of his genetic makeup, combined with his innate curiosity and desire to learn, than the junior-high keyboarding classes where, he says, "We all sat at a computer staring at the ceiling while the teacher walked around the room chanting '*a, a, a,* space, *s, s, s,* space."

As you can see, when evaluating your child's school, you need to be aware of a great deal more than its academic standing. The local newspaper may report its test scores and perhaps the purchase of new computers, but if you're intent on a well-rounded education for your child—one that enriches him intellectually, physically, socially, and emotionally—you'll look beyond test scores and technology. You'll do what you can to ensure he has access to the arts, physical education, and recess.

Don't Forget

- Developmentally appropriate means matching children's learning experiences to what we know about how children learn and develop.
- Children enrolled in play-based preschools do *not* have a disadvantage over those enrolled in preschools focusing on early academics.
- Children who experience early academics in lieu of play tend to be more anxious and less creative.
- A young child is not developmentally ready for traditional academics.
- Play promotes a wide variety of skills necessary for success in school and life.
- There's no need for children under seven to be exposed to computers.
- A well-rounded education addresses the whole child and includes physical education, recess, and exposure to the arts.

6 ★ Finding the Right Organized Activity Program

"*I tried to enroll Bella in ballet, and after the first class, she just didn't want to go back.*"

—(La Reine, mother of a four-year-old)

"*Both of our children are in tae kwon do. We chose this particular school because . . . I've watched many, many classes, and I've seen how wonderful [the instructor] is with the kids. If he wasn't, we wouldn't be there.*"

—(Shannon, mother of a six-year-old and an eight-year-old)

"*Brendan was in baseball for one season and hated it. When he didn't want to be in baseball the next season, I told him that it doesn't really matter if he plays unless he plans to be a professional someday!*"

(Lorrie, mother of an eight-year-old)

These statements demonstrate some of the ways parents choose activities for their kids. Sometimes it's trial-and-error (in one case, it took only one session for the activity to be discarded; in the other, it took a whole season). Sometimes it's a matter of extensive research. In all of the instances above, the parents involved gave careful consideration to their children's needs, including the need to quit.

The preceding chapters may have led you to believe that I'm opposed to all organized programs for children. I'm not. Developmentally appropriate organized programs can offer children and parents opportunities for socialization, and those involving physical activity can ensure that children have the chance to regularly play and move. What I do object to is the assumption that only by enrolling our children in organized programs can we do right by them. I also object to the false claims made—either brazenly or subtly—by many sponsors of these programs. Too many of them promise that they'll improve children's athletic abilities or physical prowess. And it concerns me that some parents register their children without considerable thought as to what they really want their kids to get from the experience, or have improbable expectations of what their kids will accomplish.

As I've noted throughout this book, your child will not suffer for lack of organized programs. But should you wish to enroll your child, I can alert you as to what to look for in a program—both sports and other physical activity programs—and I'll do so in this chapter. We'll also address parental expectations. What is it you're hoping for when you sign your child up? Is it within reach? And is it what's best for your child? Finally, we'll explore some of the issues that will be relevant once your child is actually participating in a sport.

What Should I Look for in a Program?

Even if your little one is too young for organized sports, you may still want to participate in some kind of structured physical activity program. You may be looking for regularly scheduled opportunities for you and your child to socialize—to get together and have fun with other parents and children—or to set aside a certain time each week where physical activity is guaranteed. If so, you won't have any trouble finding programs from which to choose. The difficulty may lie in choosing the right one.

Many centers, in the tradition of playgrounds, provide space, equipment, and opportunities for moving and socializing. Some offer Mommy/Daddy-and-me "classes" for babies and toddlers. Some offer drop-off programs for preschoolers. The latter type should have a small participant-to-instructor ratio (no more than ten children per adult). With any kind of program, the instructors should be well trained, with special understanding of early childhood. The equipment will be child-sized, yes, but they should also be of the types that were originally created with children in mind. That means there are no treadmills or barbells—no pieces initially designed for adults but later miniaturized for children. Finally, the program must have a philosophy of fun first—of *play*, as opposed to regimen.

Beware of programs that promise to improve your child's physical prowess, "accelerate" his skill development, or get him "pumped up" (increase his muscle strength). The first two aren't physically possible. The final promise is somewhat of a possibility, but generally strength training isn't appropriate for children under twelve (primarily because the bodies of younger children are not yet fully developed). Even if getting pumped up were a possibility, because fitness is fleeting—an ongoing process, as opposed to a finished product—any pumping up gained will be lost as soon as your child stops working at it.

If your child is still a baby, it's best to avoid infant exercise programs that call for working your little one's limbs. The American Academy of Pediatricians (AAP) warns against programs in which a baby's limbs are exercised, held in various positions, or otherwise manipulated. Naturally, you wouldn't intentionally push beyond your baby's limits. Still, it's all too easy to do, and pediatricians are seeing more fractures and muscle strains as a result of programs like these.

Before making a decision, visit the centers you're considering and bring your child with you. If the program is intended for infants, the emphasis should be on ensuring one-on-one time between you and your baby, during which you gently play and move together. If your child is older, ask yourself which programs look like the most fun. Which offer a balance between structure and free choice for the children? Are their goals developmentally appropriate? How well do the instructors interact with the children? Most important, which program is your child most enthusiastic about?

Does Your Child Want to Participate?

As the parent of a young child, you're used to the responsibility of making appropriate choices for her. As the adult, you must decide whether or not to enroll her in preschool, on which days she should don outerwear, and what holidays you'll celebrate and how. You're responsible for choosing the foods she eats, the time she goes to bed, and when to schedule doctors' visits. Children, of course, can't be expected to make these decisions for themselves. If allowed to do so, they might well choose to eat nothing but chocolate, go to bed at the same time you do, and skip the doctors' visits altogether.

However, when it comes to participating in sports, the most significant consideration is your child's desire to do so. The choice must be primarily his. Has he expressed interest in participating in sports or another organized activity? Is there one in particular that appeals to him?

As mentioned briefly, people who are required to do something that isn't their choice will frequently stop doing it as soon as the choice is theirs to make. Of course, this includes children. Conversely, because choice is a major ingredient in intrinsic motivation—and intrinsic motivation fuels even the youngest people—having some say in what you will and will not do makes it far likelier that you'll continue doing it! In children, having choices also contributes to the development of autonomy. Besides, studies have shown that children who participate in sports only to please their parents have higher levels of stress.

Which Activities—and How Many?

"My four-year-old son plays soccer, takes swimming lessons, is enrolled in Ju Jitsu, and has been taking a gymnastics class for two years. My two-year-old daughter swims, takes gymnastics, and cheers her brother on at his other activities . . . Kids like to be active. It's part of their nature."

—(Serena, a blogging mom)

It is part of children's nature to be active and energetic. But being active and energetic in organized programs is a fairly recent phenomenon. And as I pointed out in an earlier chapter, most children aren't enrolled in programs because they've expressed a desire to be; they're enrolled because their parents have signed them up.

In choosing activities for your child, the decisions should begin with your child's wishes. *In what has he expressed interest? What kinds of activities does he enjoy?* It is by following your child's lead—by pursuing those activities that appeal to him—that you and he will discover where his eventual talents and passions lie.

Know this, though: those talents and passions are unlikely to show themselves in early childhood. There are very few prodigies in this world. And children change. Not only will her physical size and attributes continue to alter significantly; her interests and passions will vary as well—if not from month to month, then from year to year. That's the way it's supposed to be! Children are, by nature, dabblers. From birth, their lives are about exploration and discovery. Everything new is exciting to them. However, not everything that initially excites them is going to stick. If it did, they'd have a heck of a time finding their direction in life.

Of course, you want to raise a well-rounded person. And trying different activities during childhood and adolescence helps promote a well-rounded child—in all domains of development. Knowing that, you might be tempted to let him participate to his heart's content. But my recommendation at this stage of his life is this: remind yourself that, given the option, your child would probably also choose multiple desserts after dinner. Therefore, as the adult, you're going to have to set the same kind of limits: one at a time. With organized activities—whether we're talking about sports, foreign-language lessons, or dance or piano classes—that translates into one per season. Even then, you'll need to consider the time commitment involved. As you'll read in chapter 9, the commitment for something like Pop Warner football can rival that of players in the NFL. So you'll want to choose judiciously. For children eight and under, I recommend a maximum of two sessions per week and a *maximum* of two hours per session.

If you think your child has a special talent—say, in tennis—but she expresses a desire to sign up for another activity (swimming, for example), you can rest assured that experience in one activity won't detract from experience—or even developing superior talent—later in another. Many a professional athlete has pursued one sport early in life, only to discover in later years that he feels more strongly about—or is better suited to—a different one.

REALITY CHECK ✓

- Hakeem Olajuwon, often called one of the greatest centers in NBA history, started his athletic career playing handball and as a goalie in soccer. He first played basketball at age fifteen.
- Olympic track star Jackie Joyner-Kersee was a talented basketball player in college.
- Deion Sanders, probably best known for his fourteen-year NFL career, also played professional baseball and was an All-State basketball player in high school.

How do you decide which activity to start with? After determining your child's interests, consider your child's strengths. Do they match her interests, or are they unrealistic for someone at her stage of development? Is she more physically developed than socially mature? If so, she's probably better suited to individual sports, like karate or gymnastics, than team sports, where cooperation is key. If she isn't yet emotionally ready to handle losing, something like noncompetitive swimming may be the sport for her. If she thrives among others but is small for her age, or not especially coordinated, she may be better suited to something like T-ball, as opposed to soccer, with its strenuous physical demands.

REALITY CHECK ✓

Children under the age of eight should not pitch baseballs, as they risk injury to their elbows as well as to the batters. Children under twelve shouldn't play regular football due to the potential for injury when blocking and tackling.

Look at your child's physical, social, emotional, and cognitive development objectively. These domains of child development rarely progress at the same rate. Even if they did, it would still be true that every child has strengths and weaknesses. The more clearly you can see your child's, the better you can help him make good decisions.

Finally, should you detect one special interest or talent, resist the temptation to let him specialize—pursue one sport to the exclusion of all others. If you find you're leaning toward the "Tiger Woods thing," remind yourself that there are far more famous athletes who got considerably later starts (some of whom are listed in chapter 2). And as also mentioned, there's no evidence that children who start earlier have an advantage over those who don't—but they do run a risk of overuse injuries and early burnout. The experts (including the AAP) advise that children not specialize in one sport until they are at least twelve or thirteen years old.

★ SUPERKID ALERT! ★

Myth: To achieve Tiger Woods's kind of success, children must specialize early.

Reality: Tiger Woods was a rare exception, and specialization can cause early burnout and keep children from discovering their true passions and talents.

Early specialization is a bad idea—for many reasons. Children who don't get the opportunity to dabble and are instead encouraged to focus on one activity become solely identified with that activity—at a time in their lives when it's just too soon to label them. They often feel valued for what they do—pitching, gymnastics, dancing, or playing tennis—rather than for who they are overall. They come to think of themselves only in this way—as the pitcher, the gymnast, the dancer, or the tennis player—and other parts of their personality remain undeveloped. Perhaps even other, more natural talents go undiscovered.

If your child has a gift, don't worry; it won't go away just because you don't pursue it to the exclusion of all other activities. Conversely, if your child doesn't happen to have been born with a special athletic talent, there's nothing you can do to instill one in him—because it's just not possible to *create* a superstar. Below are some of the developmentally appropriate organized activities available to children under eight:

T-ball. T-ball is one team sport that doesn't require children to have an understanding of the team concept. The players are four to eight years old, and there is generally no score kept for children under six. Every player bats and plays in the field, and an inning is over (there are only four of them) when all of the players have batted once. Of course, the game is named for the fact that the ball is hit off a batting tee, which means there's no pitching. Bear in mind that hitting a ball off a tee still requires hand-eye coordination, which isn't fully developed until nine or ten. If your child's hand-eye coordination isn't her strong suit and she has difficulty hitting the ball, you may want to consider a different activity. For additional information, visit www.teeballusa.org.

Swimming. Although infant swim programs are highly popular, the American Academy of Pediatrics maintains that children aren't developmentally ready for swimming lessons until they're four years old. Although they may be able to perform elementary swimming motions at about twelve months, these motions are more along the lines of a dog paddle than a traditional swimming stroke. And as with other skills learned before children are developmentally ready, aquatic skills take longer to learn and are limited by the children's neuromuscular capacity. Furthermore, according to the AAP, starting early doesn't translate into "a higher level of swimming proficiency compared with those taking lessons at a later age." If you're considering swimming as an individual sport for your child, take a look at the AAP's publications on the subject. They're available at www.aap.org.

Dance. There are so many possibilities here. But what you want to remember is that dance *technique,* in the form of ballet or tap, is generally not suitable for young children, as it's too structured, and most children under eight are not developmentally ready for the rigid adherence to form that these dance styles require. Rather, you should look for classes advertising creative movement or creative dance. Either will offer your child the opportunity to explore the many ways it's possible to move, to express ideas and personal feelings, to learn more about himself and others, and to make connections with different art forms and the rest of the world.

Gymnastics. Like ballet, Olympic-style gymnastics are considered too advanced for children under eight. If you want to enroll your child in a gymnastics program, you should look for one offering *educational* gymnastics. While Olympic gymnastics is stunt-oriented—and the ability to execute the required stunts determines success or failure—educational gymnastics is child-oriented and a natural progression of the exploration of fundamental movement skills. It's use of exploration and discovery allows children to progress at their own pace—and thus to experience much success in body management.

Music Classes. Again, there are numerous possibilities to choose from. Most developmentally appropriate are programs like Gymboree's and Music Together, both of which emphasize parent involvement and offer children opportunities to experience the elements of music through movement, singing, finger plays, and instruments. Programs like these are available for infants through preschoolers.

Should You Enroll Your Child in a Health Club?

As old-fashioned neighborhood play has diminished, physical activity programs for children have proliferated. Some, taking advantage of the burgeoning childhood obesity crisis, offer children's versions of adult gyms and health centers. Today it's not just adults who are paying to exercise; children are, too. In fact, according to the International Health, Racquet & Sportsclub Association, health club memberships for six- to eleven-year-olds in this country went up more than a third—to 1.8 million—from 1999 to 2004.

While six is a young age at which to belong to a health club, it's not even the earliest starting age for membership in such organizations. Many centers offer child-sized barbells, treadmills, and rock walls for children three and up.

But young children don't need these types of special programs and fancy equipment to promote their physical fitness. If they are given the time and encouragement to run, jump, and *play,* children will typically be plenty fit. They'll also have a lot more fun getting and staying fit. As

I've mentioned before, if something isn't fun for young children, there's little reason to do it. And while your son or daughter may at first think it's fun to be exercising like the grown-ups, in a place where the grown-ups work out, that attitude is not likely to last, as children are not physically, emotionally, or cognitively ready to exercise as we adults do.

PLAY & LEARN ACTIVITIES
Fitness Fun

If your child doesn't seem to be playing vigorously enough to promote fitness on his own, here are a few ways to get things started yourself:

- Put on an energetic CD and boogie with your child, or choose a lively march and hold a "parade" around the inside of the house.
- Play a game of "Gotcha!" chasing him around the living room or yard.
- Go outside and blow bubbles for him to chase.
- Park the car far from the supermarket or mall entrance, grab hold of your child's hand, and make a run for it.
- Whenever possible, buy movement-oriented toys, like hula hoops, jump ropes, and roller skates.

Research clearly shows that the most active children are those whose parents encourage them to be active!

Here are some of the reasons why fitness clubs—and programmed exercise regimens—aren't developmentally appropriate in early childhood:

- Young children aren't made for long, uninterrupted periods of strenuous activity. Expecting them to participate in twenty- or thirty-minute organized routines is impractical and could easily create a lifelong distaste for all physical activity.
- Children under the age of eight should not be using weights or machines—child-sized or not. Only children who are mature enough to follow specific instructions and understand the risks and benefits of strength training should be handling strength-training equipment.
- Young children aren't motivated to exercise for the same reasons that adults are. Because they live completely in the present, they don't comprehend exercising for the sake of health (that would mean looking ahead to the future, which they're incapable of doing). And we certainly don't want to encourage them to exercise in order to look good! Emphasizing exercise for the sake of appearance devalues physical activity and places too much value on appearance, which can create body-image issues.
- If physical activity is something your child has had imposed on him, he's likely to stop doing it as soon as the choice is his to make. Far better to allow him to choose his physical activity opportunities. That way he'll be more intrinsically motivated to continue.

Children who are enrolled in health clubs may come to think of physical activity and fitness as things they have to *go somewhere else* to get. The possibility then exists that as she gets older and life becomes busier, she'll eventually be unable to find the time to go to a health club or gym. Your child should know she doesn't have to go out of her way to move!

What to Look for in a Sports Program

Let me start by saying that in many cases the components of a sports program for children under the age of eight should be considerably different from those of a sports program for children in middle childhood and older. Here are some important questions to ask:

Is the program inclusive?

To begin, there should be no tryouts before the age of eight—for reasons related to readiness, outlined in chapter 2. A child who isn't ready to succeed at her first tryout isn't going to be inclined toward a second one. In fact, failure at a tryout is likely to affect your child's perception of her physical competence, and research has shown that children with lower perceptions of physical competence participate in less physical activity overall.

Here's where those parental expectations come into play. If you're enrolling your child in a sports program, you're probably doing so because you want him to have fun, get some physical activity, improve his motor skills, and learn to work with others. But none of those benefits are likely in a program involving tryouts—because a program looking for the best players will only *play* the best players. Which brings us to the second point: participation for all.

Will every child have an opportunity to participate?

In a developmentally appropriate sports program for young kids, there are no benchwarmers! For example, the American Youth Soccer Organization (AYSO) mandates that every player on every team plays at least half of every game. (In fact, their only criteria for playing are interest and enthusiasm.) A great program will also give every child a turn at every position—to ensure maximum participation, a more well-rounded player, and more fully developed skills. This philosophy also allows for the discovery of a child's greatest strengths.

Are the kids having fun?

What do you observe when you watch a game or practice? The emphasis in any physical activity program should be on *fun first*. In early childhood, not only does that mean actually playing, but it also means there's no winning and losing. That's partly because losing feels lousy, and it's just too early in life to subject kids to that. Winning is also a "product" and an adult concept and therefore of no consequence to little ones. Primarily, though, it's because young children are not yet developmentally ready to handle competition. As mentioned previously, typically children don't fully understand the process of competition until around fourth grade, and the team concept begins to develop between the ages of nine and thirteen.

Do kids learn to cooperate?

In keeping with the idea of "fundamentals first," children must initially learn to cooperate (the cooperative activities throughout this book can help with that). After all, teamwork—especially when it involves efforts to succeed over another team—involves cooperation. Once children are old enough to participate in competitive games, it will be those who best learned the principles of cooperation who will come together to make up the most successful teams. So when you're looking for a sports program for your child, not only do you want to find one with games that don't focus on winning and losing; you also want to find one that includes cooperation in its repertoire of skills taught. For example, it's the wise coach who understands that young children aren't ready to throw and catch like their older counterparts and instead invites them to practice in two side-by-side lines facing each other. The ball starts at one end, on one side, and is gently tossed back and forth to every child down the line.

Does the program teach fundamental skills?

You want to ensure that the program in which you enroll your child teaches the children to successfully execute the skills used in the sport! For example, if the sport involves throwing and catching, the program should offer the children considerable opportunity to practice throwing and catching in a variety of ways—to themselves, to their teammates, and using balls of various sizes and textures. Skill development should proceed logically, over the course of the season, from least to most challenging tasks.

This will require a coach who understands the mechanics of the skills involved, as well as the limitations and capabilities of the children who are participating. As I've said before, too many programs expect children to just jump right in and play. They teach the rules but not the fundamentals. Both are critical to success, but in early childhood, fundamentals matter most.

PLAY & LEARN ACTIVITIES
Multitasking Games

Teaching children cooperative skills doesn't have to be exclusive of teaching motor and sports skills; they can be learned jointly. For example, in gymnastics, once children have accomplished log rolls individually, the next logical challenge is to practice in pairs. A game called Footsie Rolls requires children to lie on their backs with the soles of their feet touching, and to see how far they can roll without disconnecting.

Is the coach or instructor experienced?

Of course, also critical to the success of your child's experience is the coach involved. Among the questions you want to ask are the following:

- Does the coach understand early childhood development and have experience working with children of this age?
- Is he knowledgeable about the sport and able to teach the necessary skills?
- Does she provide feedback in a positive, rather than critical, way?
- Is the coach patient, rather than punitive, when mistakes are made?
- Are mistakes considered okay—a natural part of the process?
- Does the coach know basic first aid?

Depending upon the level of play, you may also want to ensure that he or she has had training in the coaching of youth sports. Organizations

Beanbag Freeze calls for children to walk around while balancing a beanbag on various body parts. They have to stop if they drop the beanbag, and they can't move again until another player recovers it for them. This game teaches balance and body control, both of which are helpful in any number of sports.

Keep It Afloat challenges partners to keep a balloon in the air for as long as they can, without either of them touching it twice in a row. This improves eye-hand coordination and visual tracking and offers practice with volleying.

like the American Sport Education Program (www.asep.com) and the National Youth Sports Coaches Association (www.nays.org) provide such training.

The National Association for Sport and Physical Education (NASPE) offers a complete checklist you can download online (www.aahperd.org/naspe). Titled "Choosing the Right Sport & Physical Activity Program for Your Child," it consists of questions relative to safety considerations, the child's readiness to participate, parents' commitment to a child's participation, and evaluation of the program. It also includes the Bill of Rights for Young Athletes. Among the principles set forth is the "right to play as a child and not as an adult." That, perhaps, is the most critical point on which to evaluate any program.

Are *You* Ready for Your Child to Participate?

For years, the question on Monday nights from September to January has been "Are you ready for some football?" The question for you at this point is "Are you ready for your child to participate in sports?" Believe it or not, your readiness is almost as important as your child's.

What comprises a parent's readiness? Well, among other things, you have to take time and cost into consideration. If either is going to be a problem—if there's even a remote possibility you won't be able to get your child to practices on time, or may have to disappoint her because you suddenly can't afford it—don't sign her up. Your child may be too young to fully comprehend commitment, but you're not, and it is by seeing you make a deal and stick with it that she'll come to understand its value.

On the other hand, although you want to take your commitment to the program seriously, you don't want to take your child's participation in it *too* seriously. That means your child's life, and that of your family, shouldn't revolve around your child's sport. Being a soccer player or a golfer will be something he does; it won't be who he is. Your child is too young for this sort of distinction, and it's never a good idea to confirm a child's belief that the world revolves around him. Children who grow up with that impression are in for a rude awakening when they venture into the world as adults—because the world revolves around no one!

At this stage of your child's life, participation should be minimal anyway, limited to one or two sessions a week. And unless it's a requirement of your child's program you don't need to be at every practice yourself. Drop her off and go run some errands, or share chauffeuring duties with other parents. If you're worried about leaving your child in the coach's hands, you've chosen the wrong program.

Setting a Good Example

Of course, there is yet another commitment you'll have to make should your child decide to participate in sports, and it's a big one. Whether attending practices or games (bearing in mind that these should not be similar to the games played by older children), you must promise to behave yourself. That means there'll be no screaming, swearing, or skirmishes (we've all heard the stories; there's no need to catalog them here). But it also means you'll refrain from coaching from the sidelines. Your child has a coach, and it's his responsibility—and his only—to offer critiques and comments. Yes, the temptation to shout out helpful suggestions is strong. But you have to resist. Trying to please a coach is about all your child can handle at this point. Trying to also please a parent is far too much pressure!

Further, your good behavior must extend to after the games as well. Focus your remarks on your child's efforts, and even on how nice it was to be out in the sunshine or to see some of the other parents and children. Concentrate on the positives. By establishing this habit now, should your child go on to be involved in actual competitions, you'll be a pro at handling wins and losses. Then your child will never get the idea from you that winning is all that matters and loss is to be avoided at all costs. Instead, he'll come to understand that both are a part of life.

What if My Child Wants to Quit?

And what if your child expresses a desire to quit? Considering that you want her to learn the significance of commitment (it's one of those qualities that belongs under the heading of "good character"), you might be reluctant to let her do so.

Naturally, you shouldn't automatically acquiesce the instant your child says she doesn't want to play anymore. A child may be too young to understand obligation, but will still get the wrong message if she gets her way with a single comment. Rather, you should explore her reasons for wanting to quit. Does she have a fear—perhaps of being hit by a ball—that you can help her overcome? Is there a skill she believes she lacks that you could help her practice?

Or is she simply not enjoying the experience? If that's the case—and she's tried it several times—then by all means let her quit. Maybe it was the wrong activity for her. Or perhaps what she needs most of all is unstructured time.

Yes, your child may have pleaded with you to enroll him in a particular sport. And it may be that only a couple of weeks—or only a session or two—have passed. But if the point of early sports experiences is to have fun and promote a lifelong love of physical activity, forcing a child to continue when he clearly and repeatedly expresses that he doesn't want to isn't going to benefit anybody, least of all your child. Furthermore, at this point in a child's sports career, if he's truly enrolled in a program that expects him to be a little kid rather than an adult, his quitting is not going to devastate the team.

REALITY CHECK ✓

The number one reason children sign up for sports is to have fun.
The number one reason they quit is that it's not fun anymore.

If you insist that your child continue with a sport despite his objections, you run the risk of: (a) alienating him, (b) invalidating his ability to make his own decisions, and (c) burnout. Even if the choice was initially his, if he worries that he would be letting you down by quitting, he'll stick with it long after the joy is gone.

Finally, if you find you're unwilling to let your child stop playing—or if your disappointment feels more like devastation—sit yourself down and evaluate your expectations once again. It may be that they were loftier than they should have been after all. Or were you hoping to live out an unfulfilled dream of your own?

If you think about it, there are thousands—if not millions—of successful, happy people who have never scored a goal in hockey or soccer, thrown or caught a touchdown pass, or hit a home run. (I have never done any of those things, and it hasn't kept me from doing what I've wanted to do in life, including writing fifteen books.) Many successful people have never even touched a baseball, soccer ball, football, or hockey stick. Most people, it's probably safe to say, didn't much care—or don't now remember—who won the local Pop Warner playoffs or Little League tournament. And their lives turned out just fine!

Don't Forget

- Young children don't need special programs and fancy equipment to promote their physical fitness; they just need to engage in active play.
- Programs offering physical activity for young children should have small participant-to-instructor ratios, well-trained instructors with an understanding of early childhood, and equipment originally created with children in mind.

- Beware of exercise programs for infants and programs that promise to "pump up" a child, accelerate motor skill development, or improve physical prowess.
- The choice of whether or not to participate in sports belongs to the child.
- Young children should only participate in one sport at a time—at a limited level.
- When choosing a sport with which to begin, match your child's interests with her or his strengths.
- Children should not specialize in a sport until they are at least twelve or thirteen years of age.
- Whether it's a physical activity or sports program, the primary focus should be *fun!*

7 ★

You've Gotta Have Heart
Why Compassion
Matters More than Competition

"I can remember when I first began coaching in a traditional sport program and saw the bewilderment in children's expressions when adults encouraged them to cheat or purposely injure an opponent. It was equally memorable how quickly children adapted to these expectations. It didn't take too long before these same children would brag about how they cheated or injured an opponent. By high school age, many had turned it into an 'art form' and a 'legitimate asset' in their own eyes. After all, they were getting positive feedback from coaches, parents, peers, and spectators when they got away with cheating or hurting an opponent."

(John Dutrow, director of Sport4All)

What does it mean to "build character?" To me, a person with character is good-hearted, has the courage to know and do what's right, to make the tough decisions in life, and to take risks. Someone kind, generous, loving, empathetic, and altruistic. To be all of these things, a person also needs to be confident, resourceful, resilient, and motivated by internal, rather than external, rewards.

Ask any parent if she wants these traits for her child—if she would like her child to grow up to be the above-described adult—and you'll probably get a heartfelt *yes*. What I've described is a good person—a person with character. Of *course* she wants her child to become this kind of human being.

The problem is that in our quest to give our children advantages, the pendulum has swung too far in the other direction. The anecdote that opens this chapter is only one example of how children are currently being taught to *lack* character. In today's superkid culture, the message coming across—in subtle and plenty of not-so-subtle ways—is that what's most important is doing and being better than "the other guy." That what matters most is winning—at all costs. That it doesn't make a difference how you get what you want, as long as you get it. That risks (except the calculated kind) should not be taken—nothing left to chance.

These messages come across when intellectual development is emphasized to the detriment of social and emotional development. When children witness the extraordinary lengths to which their parents will go to get them into the best schools, hear adults comparing their academic achievements with those of the other kids, or are drilled on their ABCs but not on "please" and "thank you," they learn not to value "the other guy" but to compete with him.

When we overprotect children—shielding them from failure and sheltering them from mistakes—children learn that failure and mistakes are unacceptable. When children are praised and applauded not only when they excel, but also when they don't excel and when they don't even try, how are they to learn to value effort?

When adults are over-involved in every aspect of children's lives—pushing and prodding in their attempts to promote excellence, doing the children's homework to ensure high grades, and choosing all of their activities for them to improve the college résumé—children never learn independence, or to rely on themselves.

And yet, as children learn not to take chances, that other kids are the enemy (and inferior), and that they can't stand up for themselves, their parents simultaneously want their children to have the highest possible self-esteem. They fail to see the dichotomy here: that children who don't take responsibility for their good grades, playing time, and even their mistakes will never have true self-esteem.

This chapter looks at what it means to be a successful person, not in terms of having the highest academic and athletic scores, but in terms of having character—the kind of character that ensures success regardless of one's academic or athletic scores. We'll explore how to effectively contribute to your child's self-esteem in a superkid world. And why having heart is more likely to guarantee happiness in life than having your heart's desire handed to you.

The Entitlement Generation

Entitled. It's a word that appears in dozens of news stories to describe today's youth:

- An Associated Press article reflects on the vast chasm between the expectations of today's young workforce and the realities of the workplace. Its subtitle: "Employers ponder 'Entitlement Generation.'"

- The subtitle of a *Milwaukee Journal Sentinel* article reads "Excessive positive reinforcement has taught a generation that they're the center of the universe."
- In the latter article, New York pediatrician Ralph Lopez refers to "overindulged child syndrome."
- Among the examples cited in these pieces are the rejected *American Idol* contestants who were shocked and outraged by the judges' assessment that they're not as talented as they presumed, and the just-out-of-college kids who expect, at the start of a new job, the salaries and benefits typically reserved for twenty- or thirty-year veterans.

Entitlement is also a word I've used to describe some students in my university course. Over a twelve-year period of teaching, I had increasingly noticed that my students seemed to feel entitled to good grades rather than having to earn them. Although they had been serious and hardworking at the beginning of my tenure, toward the end their attitude had deteriorated to the point that they were putting less effort into getting a good grade but becoming more insistent that I give them one. If I didn't, I would receive phone calls and e-mails demanding to know why. One of my students received a flunking grade on the midterm exam and failed to do the final project correctly, but he was still stunned that he hadn't received the expected A-minus. Eventually, parents' phone calls and e-mails began replacing those of the students. One year, as I was trying to decide whether or not to return for another round, a colleague asked if teaching the class offered more satisfaction than frustration. "No!" I exclaimed, without a moment's hesitation. "There's your answer," he said. And I hung up my chalk.

Since then, as I've talked with professors around the country, I've discovered I'm not alone in my assessment of how students have changed over the years. Beyond the fact that they're no longer willing to earn their diplomas, according to one professor, students aren't joining volunteer or meaningful organizations like they used to. In stark contrast to the sixties and seventies, she said, when activism abounded and selfish pursuits diminished, membership in sororities and fraternities is currently up. In the past, this professor lamented, students joined organizations because they were interested in them— in making a difference. Today their interest lies in boosting the résumé. In other words, they're more interested in what they can gain than in what they can give.

Certainly, "overindulged" and "entitled" aren't complimentary terms, and no parent strives to raise a child who's either. But unfortunately that's what far too many parents have done. And their now-grown kids either believe that they're superior to everyone else ("What do you mean I can't sing? I'm the best singer you've ever heard!"), or they think the world owes them ("What do you mean you can't start me at three hundred thousand dollars?").

Addicted to Praise

How has this happened? Well, for the past decade, the so-called self-esteem movement has led parents to believe that plenty of praise and positive reinforcement gives children the self-esteem they need to succeed. That if repeatedly told how talented, smart, and wonderful they are, children come to *be* talented, smart, and wonderful—regardless of their efforts and actions, and sometimes despite the fact that their efforts and actions indicate otherwise. Blue ribbons are handed out to all participants at an event, regardless of performance. Happy-face stickers are placed on all homework assignments, regardless of execution. "Good job!" is the mantra of Mommy and Daddy, regardless of what the child has or has not done. One young mother even told me she never said no to her four-year-old son, because she didn't want to negatively impact his self-esteem.

★ SUPERKID ALERT! ★

Myth: Parents and other adults are responsible for giving children self-esteem.

Reality: Self-esteem can't be bestowed!

These examples may seem harmless, especially considering they make children feel good—temporarily. But there are many problems with the concept of giving children self-esteem, not the least of which is that it isn't possible. (You can foster it, but you can't offer it up like Halloween candy.) Also, trying to bestow self-esteem through constant praise and positive reinforcement simply does not prepare a child for the realities of life. *Someone* is eventually going to say no to her. Instead of a happy-face sticker, a teacher or an employer is going to hand over a heavily red-penciled report and demand to know what she was thinking. Blue ribbons will not be awarded just because she walked through the classroom or office door. And no one is going to say "Good job" unless she's actually done one. (Even then she might not hear it!) Along those same lines, a person will not be hired just because she *thinks* she's the best in the world. Nor will she receive a three-hundred-thousand-dollar salary simply because her mommy and daddy have told her she deserves it.

The self-esteem movement has also resulted in what experts are saying is a link between instant gratification ("Thanks for coming; here's your blue ribbon.") and a lack of frustration tolerance in children. In Sharna Olfman's book *All Work and No Play: How Educational Reforms Are Harming Our Preschoolers,* psychiatrist Marilyn Benoit notes that she's seeing a growing number of "explosive" children who are "unable to cope with the slightest of frustrations, and lash out aggressively. They are entitled, demanding, impatient, disrespectful of authority, often contemptuous of their peers, unempathetic, and easily wounded." This certainly describes the teenage girl I witnessed, who threw a heavy, second-place trophy at the judge who handed it to her because, to her, first place was the only ranking that mattered. Being number two wasn't acceptable, but having a temper tantrum (at her age) and possibly injuring a judge were.

When a child is convinced that he is superior to everyone else and can do no wrong, eventually reality comes crashing down—and then so, too, does the child.

Afraid of Doing Wrong

> *"Yesterday the kids came in for their first-grade music class all hot and sweaty from 'running' the quarter-mile 'race' around the bus loop. One little peanut, not bigger than a minute, said to me, 'Yeah, I failed.' I told her she absolutely did not fail—that she tried her best and that was all she needed to do. I told her she was good at so many things, and I reminded her about that great story about the tortoise and the hare."*
>
> (Jill, elementary-school music teacher)

Of course, at the opposite end of the spectrum from the kid who thinks she can do no wrong is the kid who is *terrified* of doing wrong. When a child is constantly praised for what he does—getting good grades or being the best hitter on the team, for instance—that child dares not stop getting good grades or being the best hitter on the team for fear that the praise will end. He has become dependent upon doing well, and doing so is all tied up with his self-concept. He also wants desperately to continue pleasing his parents—the most important people in his life—and fears that won't happen unless he maintains his record of "perfection."

Now, you might think that any incentive to continue being the best is a good thing, but a child who is motivated only by her parents' praise will not only be extrinsically motivated but will also be reluctant to try anything new—just in case she's not as good at it. That child becomes terrified of failing, and the pressure to be perfect often negatively affects the very things that were so important to her parents: her academic or athletic performance. That child is then unlikely to become an adult with the courage to face the possibility of trying and failing.

PLAY & LEARN ACTIVITIES
Silly Games

I've witnessed children as young as four years old who are afraid of failing or looking foolish. They're the children who sit on the sidelines during movement and music sessions regardless of how badly they want to join in the fun, who color meticulously (and fearfully) within the lines, and who won't raise their hands in class because they might have the wrong answer.

Being silly is a wonderful antidote to this kind of fear. So play a game of Twister, which invites both silliness and risk taking. See who in the family can make the goofiest face. Make up silly dances. Play a game of Belly Laughs, in which family members or several children lie on their backs and place their heads on the belly of the person next to them. The person at one end says "Ha!" The next person says "Ha-ha!" The third says "Ha-ha-ha!" And so on down the line!

There's no one right answer in these kinds of activities, which frees children to express themselves and even take creative risks. As an added benefit, my friend and colleague Jackie Silberg, author of *The Learning Power of Laughter,* tells me laughter relieves stress, perpetuates feelings of happiness and joy, diminishes pain, and boosts serotonin levels.

Decreased Motivation

Should you need even more evidence that excessive positive reinforcement can be negative, there's this: children who have been overly and falsely praised—for everything from "being nice" to reading—are less likely to keep doing whatever they've been praised for doing. Kids aren't dumb. They know false praise when they hear it. And they know they're going to receive it regardless of what they do. So why bother making an effort? An article on the Internet includes an anecdote from a new teacher who used praise lavishly as a way to "win over the group." But when he later became frustrated because the class wasn't focusing, he chided them for not putting in enough effort. In response, one student said, "What's the point? You'll just tell us we did fine anyway."

It only makes sense: when you're constantly being rewarded and positively reinforced, regardless of what you do or the effort you do or don't put forth, intrinsic motivation shrivels up and dies. And a life without intrinsic motivation—from the satisfaction that flows from *within*—means a life in which *extrinsic* rewards provide the only incentive for doing something. Why work hard at a project if there's not a significant amount of money involved? Why run the race if you can't be assured of a first-place ribbon? Why volunteer your time and energy if being helpful is the only payoff?

Kids easily become addicted to praise. The more they get, the more they need. But isn't it better for them to become addicted to the good feeling that comes from doing things for their own sake? Isn't it better that rather than being told how wonderful they are, they're allowed to confirm it themselves? To learn from experience that just like everyone else they have strengths and weaknesses—and that it's okay to have both? It makes them so much more *human*—less likely to feel entitled to anything they don't deserve and more likely to feel that they, along with the rest of the world's humans, are all in this life together. And when they succeed at something—employing their strengths and overcoming their weaknesses—they will have *earned* the pride they feel.

REALITY CHECK ✓

If parents want their children to be intrinsically motivated, they shouldn't offer rewards for things the children should want to do, like reading, keeping a clean bedroom, or playing with a younger sibling. In a presentation on the topic, Alfie Kohn, author of *Punished by Rewards: The Trouble with Gold Stars, Incentive Plans, A's, Praise, and Other Bribes,* told his audience there are more than seventy studies showing that the more kids are rewarded for doing something, the less interested they are in whatever they had to do to get the reward. Because they're thinking, "If they have to bribe me to do this . . . ," it devalues what you're asking them to do.

In *Child Development,* noted educator Bev Bos writes: "[Children] do not have to be told they are wonderful because they are born knowing they are. They are born with an inherent self that is intellectual, complete; an inherent self that can dance, sing, write poetry, and tell stories, and has a sense . . . of joy about learning, growing, and doing."

PLAY & LEARN ACTIVITIES
Fostering Intrinsic Motivation

- As an alternative to praising or rewarding your child for reading, snuggle together on the couch and read *with* him. You're modeling positive behavior and helping him associate reading with good feelings.
- When you want your children to play together, offer a small selection of games, inside or outside, to choose from. (Choice is a necessary ingredient in fostering intrinsic motivation, but having too many options to choose from can overwhelm a young child.)
- When you want your child to clean his room, make a game out of it by putting one of his favorite songs on the CD player and challenging him to pick up before the song ends. Cleanup then becomes associated with fun. If you join in, emptying the dishwasher, for example, the sense of togetherness adds to the experience.

Coddled Kids

"I walked or biked to school for years, but my children don't. I worry about the road. I worry about strangers. You can start to imagine evil on every corner. In some ways, I do think they're missing out. But I like to be able to see them, to know where they are and what they are doing."

—(Leanne, quoted in a *New Zealand* newspaper article called "Bubble-Wrap Generation: Our Molly-Coddled Kids")

In some respects, the issue of coddled kids—and the children's resulting behavior—is the same as the reports on entitled kids. Except here the focus isn't on praise, but on parents' overprotectiveness. The New Zealand article, for example, states: "What has altered quite dramatically is the confidence we once had in our children's ability to fling themselves at life without a grown-up holding their hand." And: "Child-rearing has become an exercise in risk minimisation."

Of course, it's not only in New Zealand that kids are overprotected. In a letter to the editor of the *New York Times,* in response to an article called "How We Took the Child Out of Childhood," a twelve-year-old girl writes that she doesn't know "one friend of mine that can actually walk across the street without parental supervision. . . . Parents these days are completely paranoid!"

Not surprisingly, much of today's paranoia can be chalked up to the fear factor—the terror brought about by the media's incessant tales of tragedy, presented in all their gory minutiae. But experts, including noted educator David Elkind, contend that today's children are no less safe than children of my generation. Social historian Peter Stearns agrees. Quoted in a *Psychology Today* article called "A Nation of Wimps," Stearns maintains that parents have exaggerated many of the dangers of childhood while overlooking others, like the demise of recess.

"Stranger danger" is certainly at the top of the list of parents' fears, but according to Freda Briggs, a professor emeritus in child development at the University of South Australia, stranger danger is a myth. In Australia, for example, the odds of a child under fifteen being murdered by a stranger are in the vicinity of one in four million. And according to U.S. Department of Justice statistics on violent crimes, between 1973 and 2002, out of every thousand children kidnapped, just one or two of them were abducted by strangers. In fact (and this goes to Peter Stearns's point about recess), according to the National Center for Health Statistics, children are four times more likely to die of heart disease than to be kidnapped by a stranger.

Still, parents are afraid, and their anxiety is creating anxious children who don't dare make a move on their own. The *Psychology Today* article describes today's young people as dependent, risk-averse, psychologically fragile, and riddled with anxiety.

Overprotecting Children's Feelings

Less dramatic but also having a serious impact on children is a second fear factor: parents' worry that their children's self-esteem will suffer—and perhaps their futures as well—if they should have to endure failing, losing, or making a mistake, all of which have come to be equated with disaster. To avoid this, parents often make their children's decisions for them, complete their homework, resolve their conflicts, and let them win every board or backyard game.

For example, psychometrician Kimberly Swygert's Web log, "Number 2 Pencil," relates the workforce experiences of two "coddled kids." First was the twenty-four-year-old car salesman who didn't get his annual bonus because of his poor performance. Both of his parents arrived at the company's regional headquarters and sat outside the CEO's office, refusing to leave until the CEO would meet with them. Then there was the twenty-two-year-old pharmaceutical employee who didn't get the promotion he wanted because, according to his boss, he needed to first work on his weaknesses. Because he was a Harvard graduate who had excelled at everything he had ever done, he was devastated. His parents, however, were sure they could find a way to fix it, as they had fixed everything in the past. His mother called the Human Resources Department the next day *seventeen times*, demanding a mediation session with her, her son, his boss, and a representative from Human Resources. Yes, these are extreme examples. But they're becoming increasingly common.

At the other end of the spectrum, children who are allowed to work out conflicts on their own and to fend for themselves learn independence and resilience. When trusted to take responsibility—even if that means some failure and mistakes—kids gain the courage to make decisions and the gumption to get back up again when life knocks them down.

REALITY CHECK ✓

At an annual meeting of the American Psychiatric Association, Harvard psychologist Jerome Kagan reported on his study of hundreds of infants whom he had followed for five years at that point. His conclusion was that parents' overprotectiveness creates anxious children. In contrast, he said, the children of parents who had imposed limits on their behavior did not show fearfulness. At the same meeting, psychiatrist Michael Liebowitz stated that "overprotectiveness brings out the worst in kids." Liebowitz is head of Columbia University's unit on panic disorders and said that he finds that "an unusually high proportion of panic patients report having had overprotective parenting in childhood," according to a *Psychology Today* article titled "Parenting Style May Foster Anxiety."

When kids play on their own, they learn to solve their own problems, negotiate, resolve conflicts, and figure things out. They experiment, take calculated risks, and test themselves. They are free to discover their weaknesses, as well as their strengths, and to determine what matters enough to continue working at.

Play is the only arena in which a young child gets to be in control—in charge! But it has to be child-directed, not adult-directed, play. That means the child freely chooses the activity and how it's to be done. There are no rules other than those she may choose to make up. And if something goes wrong (the square peg doesn't fit in the round hole, for example), let her attempt to figure it out for herself. *If* she turns to you for assistance, you can help her understand why, but wait for her to try before telling her it won't work and that she has to put a round peg in a round hole.

This is not to say I'm a proponent of continual failure. As with most other aspects of life, there's a balance to be achieved! It's hard to watch your child do something incorrectly and resist the urge to fix it. No one wants to see their child struggle, even momentarily! But if you refrain from "fixing" everything for him, whether it's as small an issue as telling him where to put the pegs or as large an issue as doing his homework for him, he'll learn to be self-directed. Moreover, he'll be willing to try and *try again*. He'll become resilient.

What Is Success?

One of the main principles of movement education, of which I've been a champion for twenty-six years, is that children should experience more success than failure. In chapter 3, in fact, I stated that you should scale back the challenge if you're trying something new with your child and she's not experiencing an 80 percent success rate. When I make such statements in my presentations, my words are sometimes misinterpreted as meaning I'm also a champion of the self-esteem movement. But that's not the case.

When I discuss success, I don't mean winning all the time. I'm talking about the success that is earned after trying and achieving, even if only in increments. I'm talking about the experience of making an effort and seeing results—even if it's just enough to decide that it's worth more effort. (Those of us who've tried dieting know that even seeing small results on the scale keeps us motivated to forge ahead.) I'm even talking about trying and *not* necessarily succeeding but knowing, at least, that you tried your best.

Yes, I want children to experience more success than failure. A child who tries and succeeds more often than she tries and fails will gain the poise and confidence needed to handle future losses and failures with grace. Also, continual failure teaches children learned helplessness—the belief that one has absolutely no control over the happenings in one's life and therefore there's no point in trying. Naturally, that's not a lesson you want your child to learn!

REALITY CHECK ✓

Thomas Edison experimented with *thousands* of filaments before finding the right materials to create a lightbulb that would glow brightly for long periods. Alexander Fleming discovered penicillin by accident, followed by intentional problem solving. *Fourteen* publishers rejected Grace Metalious's manuscript for *Peyton Place* before she successfully sold it. It eventually became a best-selling novel, a movie, and a television series!

When you play games with your child, you can help prepare her for life's realities—its successes and failures, its satisfactions and disappointments—by playing honestly. You may have to change the rules somewhat to suit her age or level of understanding, but you shouldn't do it just to ensure her a win. That will only teach her that rules can be altered when they don't suit her. If you win, point out some of the things she did well. And by all means, don't gloat! That will teach her that the product (winning) and not the process (enjoying the game itself) is what matters most. By the same token, when your child engages in competitive games with others, whether she wins or loses, "Did you have fun?" should always be your first question. And if you weren't present, you'll send a strong and important message if you *never* ask who won.

Success is about positive, enjoyable experiences. Trying and achieving on one's own is one of the most positive and enjoyable of all experiences! Trying and failing but still being loved unconditionally doesn't feel so bad either.

Which brings us to the issue of mistakes. Simply put, let your child know that everybody makes them and that it's okay for him to make them occasionally, too. Even you make mistakes. And if you let him see you goof occasionally ("Oops!" is a particularly powerful word), he won't feel pressured to be perfect. By the same token, if you occasionally respond to a question with "I don't know," you'll additionally send the message that even adults don't have *all* the answers. (If you follow up with "How do you think we could find out?" you'll also be promoting resourcefulness.)

REALITY CHECK ✓

Einstein said that a person who never made a mistake never tried anything new.

A mother in Spain, with whom I've corresponded by e-mail, told me she teaches her two-and-a-half- and four-year-old children resiliency, independence, responsibility, and other character traits by being lazy, selfish, and overly tolerant herself. Seem contradictory? She explains that because she's lazy, "I don't jump every time they want something, and self-sufficiency from them is highly valued. I don't carry them; they have to walk, and they have to carry their own things up to the point of their ability." Because she's "selfish," she wants peace at times during the day, so "they must amuse themselves." And because she has a high tolerance for crying: "I don't reward tantrums, and I don't jump at the first wail. They don't get their own way if they howl. I don't respond to requests in a whining tone, and nothing happens without the magic words: please and thank you."

One other thing this clever mom contends is that "all they need at this age is to play, play, play." She won't get any argument from me.

Is It Really a Dog-Eat-Dog World?

Having read the questions and comments of physical education professionals participating in an e-mail Listserv over the past few years, I have to say that the two subjects most likely to generate heated debate are dodge ball and competition—with strong feelings at either end of the spectrum. Some believe that both of these are good for kids, teaching them valuable life lessons. Others believe they're developmentally inappropriate and have no place in the children's education. There's been little middle ground. But the comment of one PE teacher, which concerned competition and did happen to fall into that middle ground, has had me reflecting since I read it. He wrote that he had eliminated most competition from his elementary PE program but not all of it. His reason, as he stated it, was: "These kids are going to have to compete every day for the rest of their lives."

It's an interesting comment, and it certainly reflects his belief that the world is "dog-eat-dog." But is it really? Is the world primarily "every man for himself?" Is it a place that requires us to prepare our children to battle, rather than belong? To clash, rather than collaborate? To see everyone else as foe, not friend?

★ SUPERKID ALERT! ★

Myth: Being able to compete in a "dog-eat-dog" world is a necessary characteristic for children.

Reality: The old-fashioned values will be more important to a child's future than winning.

I simply don't see the world in this way. After all, there aren't, for example, only six A's allotted per classroom. If kids want good grades, they'll have to work for them—not in a way that causes someone else to fail, but by doing their own personal best. If they want to get into a good college, it's the same thing. Yes, there are only so many placements at each university, but if they've put forth the appropriate effort, learned a good work ethic, and are people with character, regardless of whether they get into their first or third choice of schools, they're going to be just fine. And the same pertains when they apply for the job of their dreams. Yes, they're competing against other applicants, but it's unlikely they even know who those other applicants are and what they bring to the table. Nor can they be aware of all the factors involved in the selection process. All they can do in that situation is to, once again, be their own personal best. Physical education professor Bob Hautala writes: "On an individual basis, head-to-head competition is rarely encountered in the real world. When an applicant interviews for a job, while they may be competing against other applicants, during their interview, they do not face these other opponents, and they would not be wise to spend time putting them down. They need to show themselves and present their skills as they relate to the job."

Today's employers are looking for people who have a strong sense of self but who are also adept at teamwork. A competitive—or superior—attitude doesn't bode well for successful employment. In fact, of the top ten qualities employers are seeking, according to JobWeb, the first four are communication skills, honesty/integrity, teamwork (works well with others), and interpersonal skills (relates well to others). A competitive attitude is nowhere to be found on the list.

Research confirms that social and emotional skills are a better indicator of future success than mental ability, and employers are actually more interested in a person's capacity to work with others than in anything related to intellectual intelligence. Companies are already being forced to spend ridiculous sums of money hiring consultants to promote team-building concepts among their employees, more and more of whom are growing up with less and less social and emotional awareness.

Employers themselves must be able to deal effectively with others. There are in fact very few careers in this world that involve complete and total solitude. Even the writer, holed up in front of a computer day after day, must understand people in order to write for or about them. And that understanding is more likely to come from having worked *with,* rather than against, them.

In a research brief called "Children and Cooperation: Moving Beyond Competition," Ohio State University's Scott Scheer points

PLAY & LEARN ACTIVITY
Expressing Emotion

It's healthy for children to be able to name and express emotions, particularly in such safe environments as their homes. Invite your child to show you how her face would look if she were happy, sad, mad, tired, or surprised. How would she walk if she were happy, sad, mad, tired, proud, or scared? Acting out these feelings helps her to better understand them and begin to realize that others have them, too!

out that "from conceiving a child to sending a rocket to the moon, our successes require cooperation among individuals. When children learn how to cooperate with others, they have distinct advantages and skills at home, work, and play as adolescents and adults."

REALITY CHECK ✓

Competition is *learned* behavior and, given a choice, preschoolers prefer cooperative to competitive activities. Also, developmentally speaking, children must learn to cooperate before they can success-fully compete.

The assumption for years has been that pitting children against one another is necessary preparation for surviving in the world of college and beyond. Today, some parents have taken that belief to heart, acting as though every other child is in direct competition with theirs for everything! But behaving as though that were true doesn't prepare children for a future in which they'll have to negotiate, cooperate, and collaborate with spouses and family members, coworkers, neighbors, and other members of the local and global community. Nor does emphasizing the intellectual over the emotional prepare them to have a well-rounded, well-lived life.

When children learn to cooperate rather than compete, good things happen. When they have the opportunity to work together toward a solution or common goal, they know that each of them contributes to the success of the venture. They also learn to solve problems in creative

PLAY & LEARN ACTIVITIES
Role-Playing

Role-playing is a wonderful way to foster empathy. Invite your child to demonstrate the actions performed by people in various occupations—from the racecar driver to the carpenter, the musician to the magician, the teacher to the tap dancer. Also, what tasks are performed by various members of a family? Ask him to show you. And because empathy should extend not only to everyone but to every*thing*, ask him to depict the actions of an elephant, an eagle, a cat, a caterpillar, a dog, a dinosaur, and more. Hopefully, by asking him to imagine what it's like to *be* these things, he'll never be able to imagine a world *without* them!

and productive ways, to become tolerant of others' ideas, and to accept the similarities and differences of other children. Perhaps most importantly to parents, cooperative activities are far less likely to cause the feelings of inferiority that so often result from comparisons made during competitive situations.

Early childhood is the time when habits are formed. This is true whether we're talking about good eating habits, physical activity habits, or habits related to social and emotional issues. Good manners do not happen by themselves. The ability to cooperate doesn't just appear. Nor do resilience, responsibility, or regard for others develop without practice. Empathy (putting oneself in someone else's shoes) and altruism (the desire to help, with no expectations in return) may display themselves in babies and toddlers but still must be fostered in order to survive.

Yes, your child is going to have to compete to a certain extent in the "real" world. But the simple truth is that she's more often going to need social and cooperative skills. And when she does compete, no matter how much you may want her to, she's not going to win all the time. But if you've given her unconditional acceptance and an early sense of security, she'll be better prepared to deal with rejection and face problems head-on. And if you've fostered her empathy, altruism, resilience, resourcefulness, and intrinsic motivation, she'll find her own success.

PLAY & LEARN ACTIVITIES
Household Tasks

Young children *want* to help out. Let them! While you're cooking dinner, ask your little one to set the table or to feed the cat. When it's time to do laundry, ask her to bring you her dirty clothes. When you're washing the car, assign her to the tires. (Don't forget to say "please" and "thank you" to her.) When your child is young, it's best to do chores together, with you or with the family as a whole. That way, it's made clear early in her life that everyone's in it together. Also, it's more fun!

Make it a rule that everyone in the family has to be responsible for some of the household chores. Sit down as a family and brainstorm a schedule. This involves the child in the decision-making process and allows him to take ownership of his chores. By the way, if the end result of your child's efforts isn't perfect, resist the urge to fix it yourself. He'll never learn to be resourceful if perfectionism is the only goal, or if he knows you're always one step behind him, cleaning up his mistakes.

Don't Forget

- Parents can help their children develop their self-esteem, but they can't give it.

- Praise and positive reinforcement offered regardless of what a child does or doesn't do will not prepare a child for life's realities.

- Intrinsic motivation is the good feeling that results from doing things for their own sake.

- When children are continually praised for what they do, they become dependent upon the praise. This results in a lack of intrinsic motivation, a fear of trying anything new, and a disinterest in whatever they're praised for doing.

- Acting silly is a wonderful antidote to the fear of failure or looking foolish.

- Children learn much through mistakes and failures. If their parents fix everything for them, they can't become self-directed.

- Social and cooperative skills will serve your child better, in the past and the future, than being competitive.

8 ★ Finding Creatures in the Clouds

The Value of Downtime

"I'm a mom of three, and a grandmother of three. I also have a master's degree in individual development, and I've been in the child-care business for twenty-five years. There are a few things I've become passionate about over the years—and 'downtime' is one of them. As a poor child, raised in the fifties, I can't even remember owning a toy. We lived in rural areas and I was left to roam and wander most of the time. I always excelled in school, and have always had a curiosity for learning. I raised my children with large back-yards and swing sets and time to let their imaginations roam. Now that I'm watching my grandchildren grow, I'm concerned about the lack of time just 'to be.' When they come to visit and their time is less structured, they say they're bored. I don't think they can entertain themselves—and time to just relax and let your imagination wander is not something they value—or for that matter, are able to achieve."

—(Lynn)

During our own childhoods, no one could have predicted there would ever be a need to defend play for kids. Even a decade or so ago, the idea of campaigning for rest and downtime for children would have seemed ludicrous. But things have changed—and not just a little, but in an opposite-end-of-the-spectrum way. There are now organizations working tirelessly to advocate for play, among them the Alliance for Childhood and the American Association for the Child's Right to Play. Even the United Nations has weighed in on the subject. Article 31 in the UN Convention on the Rights of Children recognizes "the right of the child to rest and leisure, to engage in play and recreational activities appropriate to the age of the child."

Intuitively, you know that your child—that everyone, in fact—needs downtime. No one, even the most energetic among us, cares to rush through their waking hours, day after day after day. You know how stressful it is to be overscheduled, over-pressured, and overwhelmed. You've witnessed the toll it takes on adults—and you don't want to exact the same price from your child.

Still, you wonder if it's enough for him simply to engage in ordinary play and recreational activities. To spend time doing "nothing." Take a poll of parents and they'll agree that play is important for children. But even people with the strongest conviction can waver when faced with pressure from neighbors and friends who are convinced that their children's college applications will outshine all others if they just keep their kids busy, busy, busy. Naturally, you're going to worry you'll be letting your child down if you allow him just *to be*. What if his résumé looks sparse in comparison to those of his counterparts? What if he never "finds himself" because you didn't push him to try a multitude of activities? What if letting him simply play turns him into a lazy person?

Here are some other questions I'd like you to ponder:

- If children begin living like adults in childhood, what will they have to look forward to?
- What's to ensure they won't be burned out from all the pushing and pressure before they've even reached puberty?
- If we've caused them to miss the magic of childhood, what will kids later draw upon to cope with the trials and tribulations of adulthood?
- What will become of the childlike nature adults call on when they need reminding of the delight found in simple things—when they need to bring out the playfulness that makes life worth living?
- What joy will our children find as adults if striving to "succeed" becomes life's sole purpose?

In a poll conducted in 2004 among early childhood professionals, "family stress" was rated as the number one challenge to the well-being of today's children, with "hurried childhoods" ranking second. These were the only two categories identified as challenges by over 50 percent of the poll's respondents. Here are some other reasons we might want to consider more downtime for our children:

- In a 2004 *Washington Post* article it was reported that the use of antidepressants among children grew three- to ten-fold between 1987 and 1996, and a newer survey found an additional 50 percent rise in prescriptions between 1998 and 2002.

- According to one study, the number of children being prescribed antipsychotic drugs, many of which are for attention deficit disorder and other behavioral problems, is estimated at 2.5 million—a number that surged *500 percent* between 1995 and 2002.

- Preschoolers are being diagnosed as having post-traumatic stress, bipolar disorder, and anxiety disorders, among other psychiatric ailments.

- As previously mentioned, many young children's brains now look remarkably like the brains of overstressed adults, with excess levels of cortisol and adrenaline.

- In 1995 the *New England Journal of Medicine* reported that 150,000 *preschoolers* (10 percent of them two-year-olds) were taking antidepressant drugs.

- A 2006 study conducted by KidsHealth revealed that more than four in ten children feel stressed most, if not all, of the time. More than 75 percent of the children surveyed expressed a longing for more free time.

Clearly, something is wrong. In this chapter we'll look at downtime, not as a waste of time but as an essential component in your child's current and future welfare and success. I've chosen the chapter's title, "Finding Creatures in the Clouds," because it has significance in three realms. First, although it may be truer in the past than it is today, kids have always enjoyed lying on their backs and finding creatures in the clouds—bunnies, dragons, ghosts. Simultaneously relaxing, stimulating, and pleasant, cloud watching provides children with time just to be and let their imaginations roam. I hope to show you that such time can offer your child much more than pres-sure-cooker activities.

Second, the concept of finding creatures in the clouds implies an appreciation for nature. I propose that children should be encouraged to spend as much of their downtime as possible outdoors, not only because we're creatures of nature in danger of losing an essential part of ourselves, but also because the outdoors has so much to offer kids, not the least of which is stress reduction.

And, third, speaking of stress, finding creatures in the clouds is just one way children can recharge their batteries and avoid burnout and depression. Lying back and looking up at the sky helps children prac-tice the important skill of relaxation—a skill they can use throughout their lives, to ensure that the success they achieve doesn't come at a cost that's just too high.

Time to Just Be

Only this morning I spoke with a mom who told me she was feeling pres-sured to enroll her two-and-a-half-year-old in the local soccer program—a competitive soccer program. "Our town," she said, "is very much into pushing children to compete and succeed. And I know other parents are looking at me as though I'm failing my child, but I'm not going to give in to the pressure. I'm not enrolling her in all these programs at age two."

Whether it's a fear that children won't get into the college of their choice, fear that they will never find their passions, or fear that a child who isn't constantly engaged in organized activities will become lazy and unmotivated—whatever the reason, the result for the child is an overscheduled life and no time just to be. This is especially true once the child enters formal schooling. Early-elementary-age children spend in excess of two hours a week on homework, up from forty-four minutes in 1981, according to researchers at the University of Michigan. And too often they don't get started until late in the evening, thanks to their many after-school activities, which means bedtime immediately follows homework. (Even preschoolers are now being assigned homework—in part because parents want to see evidence of what their children are learning.) Nor are summers any longer about relaxing and having fun; they're about attending sports camps, computer camps, academic enrichment classes—anything that can be considered stimulating and that will also enhance the résumé. (The song lyrics may have to be changed to "Summertime, and the livin' is *busy*.")

What happens when a child's time is scheduled and programmed—directed by someone else—from morning till night, day after day? As one mother wrote to me: "If the parents work a full day and the children are in a traditional school, the child goes to care before school at around 7:30 AM, then goes to school, then goes to after-school care until around 5:30 PM. Then they have two hours of homework. If you add in one sport per season, they have two hours of practice/games once or twice a week. So the child's 'workday' is more than twelve hours!"

In addition to the stress it causes, an overscheduled, overprogrammed life at an early age assures that the child will never be able to entertain herself. Will never be able to live inside her own head. To deal with solitude or with quiet time. She may not get much of it as an adult, but for her sake I hope there will be *some*. And when there is, it would be awfully sad if she felt panicked at the idea of having to keep herself amused. If she felt she absolutely *had* to be in the company of others.

If you want your child to grow up to be resourceful, he'll have to start practicing now. That means he needs *unstructured* time and lots of it—in big, uninterrupted chunks.

REALITY CHECK ✓

Einstein said: "It's not that I'm so smart, it's just that I stay with problems longer."

The Power of Boredom

"But Mo-o-o-m, there's nothing to do-o-o!" Naturally, if free time is something to which she's unaccustomed, you will at first hear numerous complaints of boredom (likely in a whining tone). Ignore them! And don't succumb to the temptation to let electronics entertain her. Boredom is something today's children are rarely allowed to experience—because someone is always seeing to it that they don't have a chance! But boredom can be a powerful incentive. A child who's bored *has* to be resourceful. She has to solve this immediate and urgent problem. A child who is given enough time and encouragement will figure out what to do with herself. Eventually, she'll come to glory in these periods, finding all kinds of ways to use them, and the only time she'll be tempted to whine is when she's interrupted. A child who is fully engaged in a project, like looking at objects with a magnifying glass or sorting marbles by color and size, will be disappointed to learn she has to stop for dinner.

Boredom, along with quiet time, will also stimulate your child's

PLAY & LEARN ACTIVITIES
Counteracting Boredom

Initially, a child who hasn't had enough practice in self-sufficiency is going to need your help generating ideas of things to do. Here again you can offer her choices, but keep it to a minimum of two or three so she doesn't feel overwhelmed by the decision making. Point out that she has a new book waiting to be read. Offer to get her set up for finger painting. Or ask if she would like to help you with something you need to get done—making cookies or raking the leaves, for instance. If none of these choices appeal to her, stay your course. If you assure her that you have every confidence she can find something to do, she may initially be stumped, but because she'll want to validate your belief in her, she'll find something.

Boston Globe parenting columnist Barbara Meltz suggests that the two of you sit down sometime to brainstorm a list of activities your child enjoys. If you write them on slips of paper and put them in a jar, the next time he's bored he'll have plenty of ideas to choose from. And having helped create the list, he'll take pride in it and feel empowered.

creativity. Imagination and creativity—ideas—arise from having time to think, to ponder and reflect, or just let the mind go. A child with time to think will make up games, create dramas to act out, build a fort, or even remember where she put that lost book. A child without such time develops only the ability to do what he's told, when he's told to do it. And that child isn't likely to become an adult with initiative.

Boredom, rather than a parade of organized activities, is also more likely to help your child find her strengths and weaknesses, her passions and talents. Throughout this book, I've talked about the importance of "dabbling." As she experiments with a variety of activities at her own pace and in her own way, she discovers her likes and dislikes. And when she has the opportunity to spend time on those activities she likes—to delve deeper into the possibilities—her interests and skills blossom.

Of course, it's natural for you to be concerned if your child seems to lose interest in something after a while and then moves on to something else. But don't be. We've all had the experience of being passionate about something during certain periods in our lives—knitting, gourmet cooking, or gardening, for example—only to find these interests eventually fade. All it means is that the interest no longer serves our lives. But it definitely wasn't pointless. All of our experiences enrich us in some way. And children are meant to be fickle! Their whole early lives are about finding and losing interest, trying and discarding. Unfortunately, our superkid culture has convinced parents that this isn't a good thing—that children need to specialize early and for the rest of their lives if they're going to succeed.

Having downtime will allow your child to dabble. Free time also allows your child time to just be, and to engage in authentic play (self-chosen, self-directed, and without extrinsic goals)—alone and with others. And once she's become familiar and comfortable with the experience, rather than boredom, she'll display an amazing level of concentration as she plays. Human development expert Joseph Chilton Pearce, whose passion has been the "unfolding" of intelligence in children, calls authentic play "a state of being." Poet laureate Donald Hall says play is about "absorbedness." (Have you ever had the experience of being so engrossed in something that when you finally looked up from it, you were amazed at how much time had passed?)

Whatever this aspect of play is called, it can't happen unless your child has the time and the space with which to make it happen. Then he'll have the chance to indulge his curiosity and spontaneity. Because play employs divergent thinking, his creativity and problem-solving skills will grow. If he has the time to carry out his plans and bring them to a conclusion, he'll experience the satisfaction that comes from thinking things through and working them out.

REALITY CHECK ✓

Rebecca Isbell, early childhood educator and author, says that the chunks of time children need for uninterrupted play will vary according to their level of development. Toddlers, she maintains, require a minimum of thirty minutes to remain in play activities that interest them. Preschoolers need forty-five to sixty minutes. And early-elementary-age children who are focused on their play may need an hour or more to bring their work to a conclusion.

Take It Outside

What are your memories of childhood? Chances are good that many of your fondest memories are of experiences that took place in the outdoors. Did you have a favorite climbing tree, or maybe even a tree house?

Do you remember learning to ride a two-wheel bike, or to stand and glide on ice skates without wobbling? Do you remember snowball fights, splashing through the sprinkler, or jumping into piles of leaves? Did you hold dandelions under your chin to see if you liked butter? Were there family outings to the mountains, the lake, or the ocean? Was there a hill in the neighborhood for rolling or sledding down? Or was playing hopscotch, hide-and-seek, or cops and robbers your favorite thing?

To me, one of the saddest results of our superkid culture is that children no longer have as much time to spend outdoors. And I'm not even talking about the seemingly unlimited time my friends and I had. We had twice-daily recess on school days, and once the last bell of the day rang, there was never any thought of being indoors. On weekends and summer days, we ran out of the house first thing in the morning, hollered for the next-door neighbor to come out to play, made quick trips in for lunch and supper, and then reemerged until darkness and our moms forced us inside.

Today's children spend *little or no* time outside. With studies showing that children spend from thirty-six to forty-four hours a week with electronics (one boy, quoted in Richard Louv's *Last Child in the Woods,* said he preferred the indoors because that's where the electrical outlets are), there's little time left for being outdoors. Also, more and more kids' lives are too overscheduled for free outdoor play. When they're not attending an organized class or program, they're busy with homework, being drilled with flashcards, or "learning" on the computer. And because school is now more about seatwork and meeting requirements for standardized tests, they're lucky if they get fifteen minutes of recess a day.

As a result of all this indoor activity, today's children experience little about nature firsthand. Reports indicate that fewer than 10 percent of U.S. children currently learn about nature from being outside. Instead, one-third of them learn about it at school, and more than one-half of them learn about it via such electronic devices as computers and television!

Surely you don't need me to convince you that books and electronics offer no substitute for the real thing. Being outdoors is an experience of the senses (which is how much of young children's learning takes place). Outside there are myriad amazing things to see: creatures in the clouds, hummingbirds hovering, and four-leaf clovers. To hear: birdsong, leaves rustling in the breeze, brooks babbling. To smell: lilacs, the rain-soaked ground, and Concord grapes. To touch: the velvety softness of a petal, a fallen feather, the bark of a tree, or mud puddles. There are even things to taste, like newly fallen snow or a freshly picked raspberry. And if you recall, the simplest foods taste better outside. Somehow, a peanut butter sandwich is just a sandwich when it's eaten in the kitchen, but make it part of a picnic, and suddenly it's special.

Of course, if T-ball and soccer are among your child's multitude of activities, you may believe she is indeed spending plenty of time outdoors. And while it's true she may be getting fresh air and sunshine, both important things, such organized activities don't usually allow for the appreciation of nature that outdoor experiences are meant to provide. Heaven forbid a child should be tracking a caterpillar's progress when the ball comes her way!

Richard Louv has coined the phrase "nature-deficit disorder." He

PLAY & LEARN ACTIVITIES
Car Games

If I had my way, I'd ban all DVD players from vehicles! They promote the idea that being electronically entertained is more important than families talking to one another, and more important than taking in the surroundings, no matter how beautiful they may be. The next time you're on the road with your family or child, fill as much time as you can with conversation. When that runs its course, play a game of I Spy (for example, "I spy something that begins with the letter *f*," for field or flowers). Whoever guesses what the other person has in mind gets to start the next round. Not only does this draw attention to what's outside the vehicle's windows, but it also reinforces letter awareness. To promote color recognition and appreciation, challenge passengers to see how many green, red, blue, or yellow things they can find. And when the conversation and games run out, don't be afraid of a little quiet time. It'll give your child a chance to think or simply rest.

maintains that as children spend less and less of their lives in natural surroundings, "their senses narrow, physiologically and psychologically, and this reduces the richness of human experience."

I can attest that living in the heart of New England, where the trees perform a miracle every autumn, there are people who simply don't see it—either because they're in too much of a hurry or because they've never learned to appreciate nature.

PLAY & LEARN ACTIVITIES
Outdoor Ideas

If concern for your child's safety is keeping her indoors, remember that any time you set aside to play with her can be spent outside. Sometimes it's just a matter of playing outdoors the games you would have played indoors, like Follow the Leader or the Mirror Game (see page 48). Sometimes you can take advantage of special elements afforded by outdoor settings. For example, an outdoor obstacle course can involve such natural elements as a fallen log, a copse of trees, or a small mud puddle. If the sun is shining, make a game of trying to tag your shadows.

Indeed, to be human is to be part of nature. We evolved in the outdoors! And as much as we may have changed since our days as cave dwellers, our brains are still hardwired for an existence in nature. We therefore have an innate link with it that, when broken, leaves a part of us bereft.

Moreover, nature plays a major role in our aesthetic sense. Ecologist Stephen R. Kellert writes that the development of this sense is "instrumental in a child's emerging capacity for perceiving and recognizing order and organization, for developing ideas of harmony, balance, and symmetry." This is in addition to the primary benefit of our aesthetic sense: the heightening of our sense of beauty.

As Richard Louv writes: "When we deny our children nature, we deny them beauty." Witnessing a sunset. Letting go of the rope swing and landing with a splash in the water. Plucking a bright red apple from

And if there's a slight breeze, it adds an extra element of challenge to chasing bubbles.

Also, in the same way you arrange play dates for your little one, you can trade off with other parents who are willing to supervise the children's outdoor play. Or in the same way you hire a babysitter for evenings out, you can hire a daytime "play attendant" when there isn't an adult available. It's important to remember, however, that sometimes you or others who are present to supervise the children's safety should remain quietly in the background, allowing the children authentic play. Or if you're going to be part of the play activities, the children should be the ones choosing and directing them.

a tree and sinking teeth into its crisp juiciness. Making angels in the snow. Lying in the grass. These are immediate, sensual experiences that enrich our lives in ways we simply can't measure.

To deprive children of such experiences is to deprive them of health. Outdoors, children have the opportunity to practice and refine their emerging motor skills and to burn calories—an excellent and easy antidote to overweight and obesity. Performing large-muscle skills, like running and jumping, also strengthens bones and muscles, improves aerobic endurance, and stimulates growth of the heart, lungs, and other vital organs. Additionally, research has found that spending time in nature reduces stress, enables children to be less affected by stressful situations, and alleviates some of the daily pressures that can result in depression. And as mentioned previously, the outside light triggers the synthesis of vitamin D.

Finally, when we keep children indoors, we convey the message that the outdoor environment is of little significance. How, then, are children to learn to care for the environment? Why would they work to preserve something that they've been taught to disregard? Considering our environment is all we have to live in (until scientists find a way for us to live on the moon), it's to everyone's advantage if our children learn to love and value it while they're young. And that entails having firsthand experience of it—not simply reading about global warming or endangered species in a book or on the Internet.

You may not immediately see the link between sending your child outside and helping him to become smart or successful. There are, as I've said, different definitions of success. But if we're to consider the practical matters (beyond the health-related ones), there's the fact that outside, children feel in control and are more likely to challenge themselves, which promotes autonomy. Outside, they are more likely to invent games and rules for those games, promoting decision making, organizational and communication skills, and an understanding of why rules are necessary. Through his senses, your child will be learning lessons that are relevant to biology, physiology, physics, and more. Simple exposure to outside light has been shown to increase academic learning and productivity. And having many and varied experiences in the outdoors will ensure that he's a more well-rounded person, with greater interests and knowledge.

However, I invite you to go back and reread those questions I asked earlier in this chapter and to remember that part of being successful is being happy—finding contentment regardless of one's situation. To be able to look at life on a daily basis and appreciate what you've been given. To really *see* the beauty around you. By giving your child every chance to be a part of the outdoors and nature, you'll be helping her create fond childhood memories.

REALITY CHECK ✔

"The world will not perish for want of wonders, but for want of wonder."

—J. B. S. Haldane

Time to Do Nothing and Relax

Time to do nothing is closely related to time to just be. The focus here, however, is on the act of relaxation, which most people are unaware is a skill that must be learned and practiced. Yet relaxation doesn't receive much consideration. Indeed, constant busyness has become such the norm that relaxation is granted about as much validity as play these days.

Again, this attitude goes solidly against our instinctive knowledge that relaxation is essential to a balanced, healthy, and happy life. You know, for example, that maintaining the same intense levels of activity and attention for extended periods is stressful. You know that when stress builds up with no outlets for release, mental and physical problems arise.

Record numbers of children are experiencing depression and burnout, and much of it goes undetected. Young children don't have the cognitive ability to understand or the vocabulary to explain what they're feeling. That means they'll often act out, or display moodiness or anger, as a way of coping. Other symptoms include withdrawal, list-lessness, or even insomnia. Children may also suffer from chronic ill-ness or injuries. They may no longer enjoy what they once found enjoyable. And primary-grade children may begin to fall behind in their schoolwork.

If you see any of these signs of burnout in your child, you should cut back on his organized activities and spend some time devoted to relax-ation. Even if you *don't* witness these signs, you'll want to be sure he knows how to relax, as it's a skill that will serve him well. And the best way to ensure that is to show him that you value it yourself—by relaxing on your own and by encouraging him to do it, too. Even better, make sure that time to relax is a standard part of every day.

TAKE A TALLY ✍

Take a deep breath and take a tally when: (a) your child shows the slightest sign of burnout or just plain dissatisfaction; (b) your child asks to enroll in another activity; or (c) you find *yourself* thinking about enrolling her in an additional activity. Add up the minutes she spends in organized activities versus free time. Make a list of pros and cons, honestly and objectively determining the advantages of her participa-tion versus the advantages of letting her have the time to herself.

Relaxation Techniques

Just before bedtime is perfect for practicing relaxation techniques. Set the stage by darkening the room, speaking slowly and softly, and moving gently. If you decide to use music to promote tranquility, choose pieces with which you're already familiar—that you've found to be peaceful and soothing. Most often that means instrumental selections (although a number of children's recordings intended for relaxation include restful lyrics). The songs should be arranged simply, with few changes in rhythm or tempo. If the music is only intended to set the mood while your child performs relaxation exercises, keep the volume much lower than if the music itself were the focus of the activity, as too much external stimulation will defeat the cause. If the music is the focus, you can sometimes encourage your child to simply lie or sit quietly with eyes closed. Other times you might suggest that your little one listen for something specific, like a certain sound, instrument, or phrase.

If you want to use imagery to promote relaxation, be sure it's imagery your young child can relate to. Show her a rag doll or a wet dishrag, or talk to her about the difference between uncooked and cooked spaghetti. Then ask her to pretend to be one of these objects. You can also paint a picture in her mind. Ask her to lie on the bed or floor and imagine, for example, that she's at the beach. Talk to her (softly) about the warmth of the sun, the cool breeze, and the gentle sounds of the waves and the gulls circling overhead. Don't be surprised if she drops off to sleep.

Learning to relax, at the very least, allows children to find a quiet place inside themselves that enables them to cope—to maintain control over their bodies and minds. Just resting is not enough; children must be able to immerse themselves in total relaxation—or as Clare Cherry, author of *Think of Something Quiet,* put it: to experience serenity. The

PLAY & LEARN ACTIVITIES
Relax!

Here are other suggestions for promoting relaxation. Because it's important for adults, too, don't just encourage your child to do these exercises; whenever possible, do them with her!

- *Being Balloons.* Breath control plays an important role in relaxation. When we inhale slowly and then exhale twice as slowly, we decrease the supply of carbon dioxide in the blood, thus slowing down the activity of the nerves and brain. To promote deep breathing with your child, ask him to pretend to be a balloon, slowly inflating (by inhaling through the nose) and deflating (by exhaling through the mouth). You'll likely need to demonstrate this yourself first.

- *Statues and Rag Dolls.* The ability to intentionally control muscular tension is also critical to relaxation. Adults do this by alternately contracting and releasing their muscles. However, because young children won't understand the terms *contract* and *release,* you can play a game called Statues and Rag Dolls. Before you begin, talk with your child about the differences between statues and rag dolls. Then alternately invite her to pretend to *be* a statue and a rag doll. This, as you can imagine, requires her to alternately contract and release her muscles. (Always end with the rag doll!)

- *Feeling Calm/Feeling Nervous.* If your child is old enough to understand these concepts, you can use this relaxation exercise instead of Statues and Rag Dolls. Talk about the fact that calm is a relaxed feeling—like that experienced just before falling asleep at night, when sitting by a lake, or while watching the sun rise or set. At such times, muscles feel loose and liquid. Nervous, on the other hand, is something like a combination of scared and worried. Your child may have worried it might rain on the day of a big outing, or perhaps he lost sight of you in a big store and felt nervous until spotting you again. At those times, muscles tend to be tight. Once your child has the idea, explain that when you say the word *calm,* he should make his body as relaxed as possible. When you say *nervous,* he should tighten up. Vary the times between verbal cues, and use the quality of your voice to invoke the proper response. Do this first with your child standing. Then repeat the process with him kneeling, sitting, and finally, lying down.

- *Melting.* Melting is a wonderful—and fun—slow-motion activity. Talk about the melting of ice cream cones, snow sculptures, or ice cubes. Then ask your child to pretend to be one of these things and to show you just how slowly she can melt.

- *Finding Creatures in the Clouds.* This can only be a relaxation exercise if it doesn't become an assignment! If you send your little one outside to find creatures in the clouds, simply make it a suggestion and, perhaps, provide a blanket for him to lie on. If you join him in the activity, resist the temptation to turn it into a contest to see who can find the most creatures. Instead, lie beside him and quietly describe what you're seeing. And if neither of you discovers any creatures, it's okay to just lie there looking.

child who learns to relax will have the ability to manage stress and therefore lead a healthier—and more serene—life. But it will also ensure a more energetic life, as stress is most certainly an energy robber. Relaxation techniques enable children to "recharge their batteries."

★ SUPERKID ALERT! ★

Myth: Downtime is wasted time.

Reality: Downtime is essential to a productive life.

Relaxation techniques even offer academic benefits. According to Al Gini, author of *The Importance of Being Lazy,* "Fatigue and the frenzy of overstimulation can block objectivity, delimit perspective, and often deaden our ability to calculate and evaluate logically." Research has also proven that stress has a negative, sometimes demoralizing, impact on the ability to learn and to take tests. Tension control, on the other hand, can help children learn better and more successfully manage stressful test taking. Indeed, there was a study of "brilliant American children," which found that one of the common factors in their lives was the fact that they spent a lot of unstructured time "doing nothing." That alone should be enough incentive for you to let your child hang out and relax!

Don't Forget

- An overscheduled, overprogrammed life at an early age will typically result in a child being unable to entertain herself or to handle solitude.

- In order to become resourceful, children need unstructured time in long, uninterrupted chunks.
- Boredom promotes creativity, problem solving, self-sufficiency, and initiative.
- Bonding with nature is instrumental to many aspects of being human, including the abilities to develop intimacy, establish social relationships, and appreciate beauty.
- Outdoor play offers children physical, personal, social, and cognitive benefits.
- Relaxation is essential to a balanced, healthy, and happy life!

9 ★ Getting Back on Track
Family First

"My son really wants to play Pop Warner football, but the schedule is unbelievable. It starts in August, and the kids have to practice five days a week, from 4:00 to 8:00. Once school starts, it's three days a week, from 4 to 7. I told him it means no family vacation this summer, and that family dinners would be impossible, but he doesn't care."

—(Lisa, mother of an eight-year-old)

This anecdote is representative of what many—if not most—families are up against these days. If you're not pressuring your children to become superkids, there are plenty of organizations that are ready and willing to step in and do the job for you. Then, because all of their friends are getting involved, the children themselves begin pressuring you. But regardless of where the pressure comes from, the result is the same: a loss of childhood and a loss of family time.

As activities are piled on, family togetherness can get the short shrift. Children's sports organizations treat little kids as though they were professional athletes, scheduling practices and games during the dinner hour, on Sundays, and even on Thanksgiving! (I once learned of a little boy being benched because he skipped a game to attend his sister's wedding!) And too often, in the quest for a promising future, parents aren't focusing on the present—on their kids' childhoods. As suggested by a survey conducted by America's Promise—The Alliance for Youth and the Gallup Organization, Americans believe that the country's number one priority should be preparing our children for the future. I contend that allowing them to have a childhood *does* prepare them for the future and will do more for their adulthood than starting adulthood too soon possibly could!

In this final chapter we'll look at the importance of putting your family first and at some of the many reasons why spending real time with your child matters more to his present and future life than academics, athletics, and achievement. We'll explore the power you have to make change happen—within your family, within your community, and even at the national level. At the other end of the spectrum, I hope to help you see that there are also many ways you should just let go of the power, and to understand that by allowing your child to experience childhood, with love and what has been called "attentive neglect," she will, miraculously, become the person she was meant to become.

Family First

Studies show that today's parents are far more involved with their children's lives than their predecessors ever were. Despite this, studies also show that today's parents are spending considerably less time with their children than parents did in the past. How can both of these be true?

In general, parents are making more decisions for their children and are overseeing more areas of their lives—like their play—than did parents in the past. However, parents are also working about a thousand hours more per year and have about a third less free time than they did a quarter of a century ago. As a result, they're actually spending less time *with* their kids. Or—although the phrase has been overused to the point that it now has little meaning—less *quality* time.

Parents have become so accustomed to balancing the many demands in their lives and scheduling their own days—trying to "do it all"—that they've subconsciously fallen into the habit of scheduling and organizing their children's lives, too. The goal of all this micromanaging, of course, is to ensure the children's success—particularly their academic success. But research demonstrates that family time is what improves children's academic performance.

Bring Back Dinnertime

Do you remember family dinners when you were a kid? A friend tells me that these family gatherings were her favorite part of the day— because of the sense of togetherness they offered and because she got to relive the whole day with her recaps. Her mother tells me she babbled continuously through meals—and that everyone in the family looked forward to it.

Family dinners on a regular basis can be a great antidote to the mad rush of daily living as well as a chance for parents and children to connect. Moreover, it is only during childhood that kids have the opportunity to sit down with Mom and Dad and share their experiences *as kids*. And it is only while their children are young that Mom and Dad have that once-in-a-lifetime chance to be parents to *children*. What better, easier way to really get to know your children, including their likes and dislikes?

Here's what research has found relative to family dinners:

- National Merit Scholars come from families who eat together at least three nights a week.
- Students who ate dinner with their families at least four times a week scored higher on a battery of academic tests than students who had fewer family dinners.
- Families that eat together eat better. They're twice as likely to have five servings of fruits and vegetables a day, and they consume less fried food and soda.
- Children who eat dinner with their families engage in fewer destructive behaviors, like smoking, drinking, using illegal drugs, or having sex at young ages.
- Children who eat dinner with their families are more emotionally well-adjusted.
- Being read to and eating family dinner together have been shown to correlate with higher SAT scores.

Family dinners provide a lot of bang for the buck, as they say. What other simple activity—other than play, of course—offers so much?

Still, to make family dinners truly effective, communication is

PLAY & LEARN ACTIVITY
Dinnertime Conversation

Need conversation starters? Play a game where you go around the table, with each family member telling one thing about their day—perhaps their favorite (or least favorite) thing, something they learned that they didn't know before, or the biggest challenge they overcame. (Parents should go first so kids get the idea.) You can also use dinnertime for brainstorming—a great cognitive activity that also promotes togetherness and a sense of belonging. For instance, consider what you'd like future menus to include, what to do over the upcoming weekend, or where to go on your next vacation. Making such decisions as a family creates a bond and helps your child feel involved in an important process.

essential. To make communication possible, there can be no TV during mealtimes! Similarly, telephones should remain unanswered. You and your children can let your friends (or colleagues) know that you don't answer the phone during the dinner hour. And if it rings anyway—well, if the promise of technology is that it will make our lives easier, we should put it to use for us: Let the answering machine pick up telephone messages. Similarly, if you can't bear to miss the news or some other show, program the VCR or the TiVo.

To ensure that the family dinner is also associated with pleasure, try to avoid scolding, correcting, or otherwise lecturing as part of your communication. If there's an issue that needs addressing, it can wait until after dinner. The same applies if a child is troubled and wants to talk about it. Let him know he's welcome to bring it up but that you'll discuss it with him in more detail immediately after the meal. Then keep your promise!

Limit Screen Time

Of course, today's technology, while often helpful, can also be problematic. If you find that your family has time to watch television, play video games, or surf the Internet but doesn't have enough time for conversation or play, you have reason to implement a "no electronics" rule. It's difficult to imagine, I know. But if you specify certain periods of the day when no electronics are allowed, your child will soon become accustomed to the idea, and your family can take advantage of those times to do something else.

A 2004 study in which preschoolers put "No TV" signs on their television sets and were rewarded for not watching resulted in a 25 percent reduction in viewing. But rewards are not necessary: closer to home, a young woman I know told me that when she was a kid, her mother removed the TV from the house every summer! As a child, she had no problem with this practice, and she became a more physically active person. Because of that, as a mom, she finds that she and her two daughters are more physically active than other young families she knows. She attributes it to her mother's no-TV rule. (For ideas on limiting television in your home, check out www.tvturnoff.org.)

Not long ago, a newspaper article told of a family's decision to do without any electronics at all for a week (which proved to be a bit over-ambitious). The father, who wrote the piece, admitted that he was the one who had difficulty adjusting, succumbing after six days to the need to check his e-mail. His young children, conversely, became accustomed to the change quite readily.

REALITY CHECK ✓

A 2005 study determined that elementary school children with televisions in their bedrooms score significantly lower on math, reading, and language arts tests. If children are going to watch TV, it's best for them to do it in common areas, at common times, with other family members.

Not sure what to do with all the extra time your family will have once electronics are out of the picture? Here are some ideas:

- Read to your child. As mentioned, this has been associated with higher SAT scores. In fact, many experts say that an adult reading to a child is the first step toward both her love of books and her literary success. When she gets older, schedule "story times" when she can read to you!
- Look at the stars. Whether or not you own a telescope, huddling on the porch or in the backyard to gaze at the stars provides a wonderful sense of togetherness, while also offering your child an opportunity to appreciate and learn about the universe. When my husband and I first moved to our neighborhood in New Hampshire, we were struck by the fact that our new next-door neighbors

had gathered outside to observe an uncommon alignment of the stars and moon (as we had). At a later date, the six of us, after setting alarms to get up in the middle of the night, got together with blankets and refreshments to witness a once-in-a-lifetime meteoric event. I do love my sleep, but this occasion stands out, not for lack of rest but for the awe and camaraderie it inspired. (To this day, those parents and their two kids comprise one of the tightest family units I know. Also, both of our families have since moved, but activities like these helped establish a lifelong friendship.)

- Do chores together! As I mentioned earlier, tackling tasks together makes them more enjoyable. You'll also teach your child a great deal about responsibility if you make him part of the family effort to keep the household running smoothly. Young children actually love being helpful, so phrasing your request as a need for help will create a more pleasant association than "assigning chores." By the time your child is three, he should be ready to handle at least one regular task, like setting the table, scooping kibble into the dog's bowl, or picking up his toys.

- Play board or card games, or physical games like Twister, Cooperative Musical Chairs, or hide-and-seek. This is a fun way to pass the time, *and* it lets your child know you value play.

- Hold a picnic—indoors or out. There's no rule that dinners have to be held around a kitchen or dining room table—or that dinners have to be the only meal you share as a family! Help create a sense of fun and adventure by spreading breakfast on a blanket on the living room floor, or taking dinner out to the backyard.

- To create a love of physical activity, make a walk or bike ride part of your daily routine.

- What's happening locally that you can take advantage of? Are there pumpkin festivals in the fall? Sledding parties in the winter? Summer fairs or carnivals? In my area we have strawberry picking in June, blueberry picking in July and August, and apple picking in September. During those in-between times in your area, visit nearby parks and playgrounds for a change of scenery. Fling a Frisbee, fly a kite, or just play tickle tag!

REALITY CHECK ✓

In one study, children ages eleven to fourteen expressed a longing for a greater sense of connection with their parents and more time to do things together. In another, 21 percent of teenagers said they were most concerned about the fact that they didn't have enough time with their parents.

Parent Power

In reading Judith Warner's *Perfect Madness: Motherhood in the Age of Anxiety*, I was saddened by her contention that in America motherhood was a lot less fun than it had been in the first few years of her daughter's life in France. Because everyone was "too busy with 'activities,'" she lamented the loss of such simple pleasures as "pushing the stroller somewhere pretty for a walk" and "spending lazy weekend days in the park with another family." As you can see, she's not asking for the moon. Rather, she feels it was these little things that brought joy to the process of parenthood (and, certainly, her daughter's childhood).

As a parent, you have a great deal of power. There's no reason why such simple pleasures can't belong to you and your family. By shifting priorities and determining that racing is no way to run a life, you can ensure there's time for strolls and lazy weekends. Seem like a tall order? I know. But it's really just a matter of starting small. As a parent, you have the power to say no to your child. You can decide to balance family time and downtime with outside activities. You can decide to abide by the recommendation of the National Association of Elementary School Principals, which is that young children participate in only one activity per season, and only if it meets just once or twice a week.

You and other parents can take a stand with organizations that seem determined to interfere with family dinners, Sundays, holidays, and vacations. Once upon a time, children's sporting events and other extracurricular activities were scheduled in consideration of these family times. If enough parents speak up, they will be again. If enough parents refuse to enroll their children in organizations that don't put family first, things will have to change.

✳ TAKING ACTION ✳

Go to the Web sites of Putting Family First (www.puttingfamilyfirst. org) and Ready, Set, Relax! (www.readysetrelax.org) to read about the community initiatives these two groups have planned. In each case, the organization calls for setting aside one night during the year with the focus on the family. Sports practices, classes, meetings, and even homework are all cancelled for the night. One night a year certainly isn't enough, but it's a start!

Lisa, whose story opened this chapter, thought long and hard about letting her son practice football twenty hours a week in August and nine hours a week once school began. And she decided that on balance it was more important for him—and her family—to have dinners and summer vacation together. Her son was disappointed, but it didn't take long for him to get over it. And Lisa knows that if he eventually wants to play football, he'll be better at it for having waited until his mind and body are ready.

It's helpful to remember that there are more of you than them. There are more families than Pop Warner teams. More parents than coaches. And as I pointed out earlier, there are more parents and educators than policy makers and politicians. Unfortunately, according to one poll, by almost a two-to-one margin, parents said they didn't feel empowered—that public officials didn't care what they had to say. *But parents comprise one-third of potential voters.* Whether you're advocating for recess, physical education, safer playgrounds, pedestrian-friendly communities, or a return to developmentally appropriate early education, politicians better care what you have to say! You might even find, on occasion, that they're on your side, as was the case when Connecticut governor M. Jodi Rell launched a statewide initiative called "No Child Left Inside," intended to persuade families and children to spend more time in the state park system.

If something matters enough to you and you put your power behind you, change can happen. As an example, a number of moms around the country have made impressive progress in their attempts to restore recess to their children's schools. In one case, two mothers teamed up to collect 750 parent signatures on a petition requesting that the school board mandate two recesses daily. They also addressed the school board and lobbied school officials. A few months later, the board agreed to extend the school day by ten minutes to make two recesses possible.

REALITY CHECK ✓

Enough individual parents throughout the country have taken up the clarion call for recess that the cause came to the attention of the Cartoon Network. They've recently launched an initiative called Rescuing Recess (www.rescuingrecess.com), which offers information and support to those who want to join this particular push for action.

As it states on the Web site of Putting Family First: "We need a community movement because it is difficult for individual parents to take back family life in a culture that defines good parenting as providing more and doing more for one's children."

✳TAKING ACTION ✳

Other organizations offering information and support for families are the Alliance for Childhood (www.allianceforchildhood.org) and Parents Action for Children (www.parentsaction.org), formerly the I Am Your Child Foundation. Visit their Web sites and others mentioned throughout this book, check out what they have to say, and then choose one course of action you'd like to start with! Among the possibilities:

- Ensuring better nutrition and wellness policies in our children's schools and communities.
- Ensuring that parents have access to flexibility at work and supports at home.
- Insisting on paid family leave for all families.
- Fighting high-stakes testing.
- Calling on educators and policymakers to pay more attention to the importance of play.

Relax!

"I was talking with my pediatrician about an ABC News report I saw about a mom with two sons in college. This mother sent her sons to-do e-mails, checked their grades, their bank account balances, and even used their personal passwords to check their student e-mail. One of her sons was in a college two hours away, and she drove there twice a month to clean his dorm room, do his dishes, and pick up his laundry! My pediatrician told me that as long as her husband lived under his mother's roof, her mother-in-law had picked up his dirty clothes from the floor where he dropped them every day— and that he had expected her to do the same thing for him when they got married. She told me that had cured her of any temptation to become a parent who did everything for her child,

and she gave me some wonderful advice: She told me to raise an adult, not a child."

—(Rachel, mother of a six-year-old)

"Extreme parenting." "Hyperparenting." "Helicopter parents." These are just some of the uncomplimentary terms being assigned to today's parents and parenting styles. The last one refers to parents' tendency to "hover." They all imply an inability on parents' part to just lighten up.

★ SUPERKID ALERT! ★

Myth: Parents bear the full responsibility for a child's future.

Reality: Today's parents worry too much!

The good news is that things *are* beginning to turn around. Many of today's parents have begun to realize that they've taken on too much—and that maybe they needn't worry so much. According to one recent study, young parents consider social and emotional development as important as intellectual development. They've decided, therefore, to focus less than their predecessors have on preparing their children for Harvard. Along similar lines, a *New York Times* article described the efforts of two families who had chosen to forego "the rush-hour drives and the dinner delays" involved in enrolling their children in local league sports. Instead, they meet in a park on a regular basis so their children, ages four to seven, can play old-fashioned pickup games. One mom explained that whoever shows up plays, and that if a child is called in to dinner, the rest of the kids simply readjust the teams. These two families—and others like them—chose to "step off the high-pressure merry-go-round of youth achievement" and instead let their children be children.

REALITY CHECK ✓

Among the famous people who were "slow starters" were Walt Disney, who went bankrupt five times before finally building Disneyland, as well as Winston Churchill, Albert Einstein, and John D. Rockefeller, who were all underachieving students. Among those who never graduated from college are Bill Gates, Walter Cronkite, Alex Haley, Abraham Lincoln, Eleanor Roosevelt, Frank Lloyd Wright, and Ted Turner.

If you haven't yet gathered the courage to step off, or to simply change course—if you still worry that your child will fall behind, or won't find himself or his path to a worthy future—perhaps you can take comfort, if not from a trust in Mother Nature, then from the expertise of those who've studied such matters. Research confirms that babies are born with the desire to learn, to discover what they're passionate about, and to achieve their goals. There is also evidence that children who haven't been over-pressured, over-nurtured, or overindulged have *greater* life skills than those who grow up having things done for or pushed upon them. And much of children's development is enhanced by play and physical activity! If you want to offer your child an

PLAY & LEARN ACTIVITIES
Slowing Down

If you have any hope of stepping off the high-pressure merry-go-round, you'll need to *slow down*. Literally. If you carry your child into preschool, put on and take off his jacket, and push him in a stroller well past the point when he can walk himself—all because your life is one big rush—you should pause to consider what your child is missing. Physical activity, motor skill development, and self-sufficiency top the list. Instead, go at your child's pace—let him set the tempo whenever possible—so he can:

appropriate running start and you choose to look for it, you will find that increasingly more information and support is available to you.

REALITY CHECK ✓

One of the fallacies of our superkid culture is that our children should be good at everything—or at least improve on those things that aren't their strong points. If they focus on the negatives (their weaknesses), however, it takes time away from what they do best. If your child has a gift for music, don't insist he also excel at sports. If he shines at math, don't insist he do equally well in language arts. Let your *child* choose where his passions lie, and the future will take care of itself. As art and social critic John Ruskin said: "When love and skill work together, expect a masterpiece."

- consider what that worker ant is doing
- try his hand at balancing along the curb
- walk backward
- listen to the wind in the trees
- watch the butterfly's flight
- stroke the pussy willows

If you slow down, he—and you—will be able to smell the roses!

Yes, your child's environment plays a role in her development. Yes, there are steps you can take to "enrich" that environment and promote her development. We've explored many of them in this book. But as you reach its conclusion, I hope you now understand that it's mostly a matter of, as the old song says, doing what comes naturally.

I like to say, "The family that plays together stays together." If you can imagine the fun and sense of togetherness that result from the activities suggested here and contrast them with the stress of rushing from organized sports to "preschool prep," you can begin to imagine why this saying makes so much sense. Putting your family first and aiming literally for a "running" start will enrich your child's life—in the present and the future—in more ways than trying to create a superkid ever could.

Don't Forget

- Family time—particularly being read to and eating dinner together—improves children's academic performance.
- Children with TV sets in their bedrooms score lower on academic tests.
- Children long for more time and a greater connection with their parents!
- By shifting priorities and taking a stand, parents can help ensure that sporting events and other extracurricular events do not interfere with family time.
- Parents comprise one-third of potential voters and therefore are a powerful political force.
- Children who haven't been over-pressured, over-nurtured, or overindulged possess greater life skills than those who grow up having things done for or pushed upon them.
- It's okay to let nature take its course!

Resources

Movement's Role in Learning

Arts with the Brain in Mind by Eric Jensen. Alexandria, VA: Association for Supervision and Curriculum Development (ASCD), 2002.

Learning with the Body in Mind: The Scientific Basis for Energizers, Movement, Play, Games, and Physical Education by Eric Jensen. San Diego: Brain Store, 2000.

Moving & Learning across the Curriculum by Rae Pica. Clifton Park, NY: Delmar Learning, 2007.

Smart Moves: Why Learning Is Not All in Your Head by Carla Hannaford. Alexandria, VA: Great Ocean Publishers, 1995.

Early Childhood Education, Standardized Testing, and Multiple Intelligences

All Work and No Play: How Educational Reforms Are Harming Our Preschoolers, edited by Sharna Olfman. Westport, CT: Praeger, 2003.

The Case Against Standardized Testing: Raising the Scores, Ruining the Schools by Alfie Kohn. Portsmouth, NH: Heinemann, 2000.

Seven Kinds of Smart by Thomas Armstrong. New York: Penguin Books, 1993.

Standardized Minds: The High Price of America's Testing Culture and What We Can Do to Change It by Peter Sacks. New York: Da Capo Press, 1999.

The country's largest organization dedicated to early childhood education and the professionals who serve the field is the National Association for the Education of Young Children. Visit their Web site at www.naeyc.org.

Computers in the Classroom

The Child and the Machine: How Computers Put Our Children's Education at Risk by Alison Armstrong and Charles Casement. Beltsville, MD: Robins Lane Press, 2000.

Failure to Connect: How Computers Affect Our Children's Minds—and What We Can Do About It by Jane M. Healy. New York: Touchstone, 1998.

Physical Education and Recess

Elementary School Recess: Selected Readings, Games, and Activities for Teachers and Parents, edited by Rhonda L. Clements. Boston: American Press, 2000.

Experiences in Movement: Birth to Age 8 by Rae Pica. Clifton Park, NY: Delmar Learning, 2004.

Organizations offering information and support include:

The American Association for the Child's Right to Play (IPA/USA): www.ipausa.org

National Association for Sport and Physical Education (NASPE): www.aahperd.org/naspe

Rescuing Recess: www.rescuingrecess.com

Children and Sports

The Cheers and the Tears: A Healthy Alternative to the Dark Side of Youth Sports Today by Shane Murphy. San Francisco: Jossey-Bass, 1999.

It's Just a Game! Youth, Sports & Self-Esteem: A Guide for Parents by Darrell J. Burnett. San Jose: Authors Choice Press, 2001.

Why Johnny Hates Sports: Why Organized Youth Sports Are Failing Our Children and What We Can Do About It by Fred Engh. Garden City Park, NY: Avery Publishing Group, 1999.

The following Web sites offer information on sports parenting:

www.sportsparenting.org

www.nays.org (National Association for Youth Sports)

www.MomsTeam.com

Games and Cooperative Activities

Games to Play with Babies by Jackie Silberg. Beltsville, MD: Gryphon House, 2001.

Games to Play with Toddlers by Jackie Silberg. Beltsville, MD: Gryphon House, 2002.

Great Games for Young Children: Over 100 Games to Develop Self-Confidence, Problem-Solving Skills, and Cooperation by Rae Pica. Beltsville, MD: Gryphon House, 2006.

The Second Cooperative Sports and Games Book: Over 200 Noncompetitive Games for Kids and Adults Both by Terry Orlick. New York: Pantheon Books, 1982.

For a comprehensive look at competition, read Alfie Kohn's *No Contest: The Case Against Competition* (Boston: Houghton Mifflin, 1992). You can also visit Kohn's Web site: *www.alfiekohn.org/parenting*.

Outdoor Play and Nature

The Great Outdoors: Restoring Children's Right to Play Outside by Mary S. Rivkin. Washington, DC: National Association for the Education of Young Children, 1995.

Last Child in the Woods: Saving Our Children from Nature-Deficit Disorder by Richard Louv. Chapel Hill, NC: Algonquin Books of Chapel Hill, 2005.

The Outside Play and Learning Book: Activities for Young Children by Karen Miller. Beltsville, MD: Gryphon House, 1989.

Family Support

Alliance for Childhood: www.allianceforchildhood.net
Parents Action for Children: www.parentsaction.org
Putting Family First: www.puttingfamilyfirst.org
Ready, Set, Relax!: www.readysetrelax.org
TV Turnoff Network: www.tvturnoff.org

Books include:

Perfect Madness: Motherhood in the Age of Anxiety by Judith Warner. New York: Riverhead Books, 2005.

Putting Family First: Successful Strategies for Reclaiming Family Life in a Hurry-Up World by William J. Doherty and Barbara Z. Carlson. New York: Owl Books, 2002.

Acknowledgments

An author's name may be the only one on the cover, but it takes many people to produce a book. Among the many I have to thank for their efforts are, first and foremost, my agent, Danielle Egan-Miller, for her belief in this project from the beginning and for her support/cheerleading throughout the process. Thanks, too, to Betsy Lancefield Lane for referring me to Danielle!

I owe much appreciation to Sue McCloskey, former editor with Marlowe & Company, who saw the value of my message and helped to launch the book. When Sue decided to become a full-time mom, the editorial reins for *A Running Start* fell to Katie McHugh, who embraced the project and made it her own. Her wisdom and perception were invaluable. Thanks also to publisher Matthew Lore for his support, and to copyeditor Jill Hughes for her discerning eye and insightful questions.

I offer my sincerest gratitude to all of the educators and parents who shared their stories with me and who believe in the power of play, physical activity, and free time.

As always, my love and thanks go to Sheila Chapman, whose longtime friendship (I'm not saying how long, Sheila) has so enriched my life and to Patti Page, a world-class listener and shopping buddy. To my husband, Richard Gardzina, who gives me unconditional love, I offer, as always, my heart.

Index